DBT Workbook for PTSD

DBT WORKBOOK FOR PTSD

Strategies to Reduce Intrusive Thoughts, Manage Emotions, and Find Calm

DR. VICTORIA A. WRIGHT, LPC, DBTC

ROCKRIDGE
PRESS

For general information on our other products and services or to obtain technical support, please contact our Customer Care Department within the United States at (866) 744-2665, or outside the United States at (510) 253-0500.

Rockridge Press publishes its books in a variety of electronic and print formats. Some content that appears in print may not be available in electronic books, and vice versa.

TRADEMARKS: Rockridge Press and the Rockridge Press logo are trademarks or reg-istered trademarks of Callisto Media Inc. and/or its affiliates, in the United States and other countries, and may not be used without written permission. All other trademarks are the property of their respective owners. Rockridge Press is not associated with any product or vendor mentioned in this book.

Interior and Cover Designer: Brieanna H. Felschow
Art Producer: Sue Bischofberger
Editor: Katherine De Chant
Production Editor: Rachel Taenzler
Production Manager: Riley Hoffman

Illustrations on pages 79, 86, 90, and 121 used under license from shutterstock.com. All other illustrations by Brieanna H. Felschow.

Paperback ISBN: 978-1-63878-493-7 | eBook ISBN: 978-1-63878-661-0
R0

For my daughters, Summer and India,
the facilitators of my trauma work and
motivation for my resolve. So blessed to
have taken this purposeful journey with you.
My love extends to the heavens and beyond.

To Stacey, "The BFF." Thank you for cleaning
the wounds of my heart when I felt broken.

CONTENTS

INTRODUCTION

Unfortunately, as the number of traumatic events in our world increases, so do our stress responses. There are terrorist attacks, health-related threats, environmental threats, gun violence, sudden financial losses, tragedies, car accidents, and, sadly, many other traumatic experiences. We are becoming more anxious and stressed as the conditions we live in continue to change in distressing ways.

While some people can work through the stress and subsequent distress of trauma with support, compassion, and time, others struggle with the residual side effects of trauma. This effect is called posttraumatic stress disorder (PTSD) and is frequently associated with our armed forces and those who have directly experienced traumatic events, such as mass shootings, rape, assault, and domestic violence. What often further complicates PTSD is a lack of understanding from family and friends, who may just think you're behaving "irrationally" or "dramatically" or "making a big deal out of nothing."

In truth, what you're thinking and feeling, and how you are responding, is a *real* concern. It's a result of your experiences and requires appropriate treatment as well as empathic support. This workbook is the start of that journey, and you are bravely, confidently taking the first step.

In my practice as a trained and certified dialectical behavior therapy (DBT) clinician, I use specific skills in my treatment planning to support the wellness of my clients, especially those who have difficulty understanding what they have experienced in past traumatic events. Many clients using DBT have then been able to employ those skills independently during moments of distress. It has helped them improve their functioning and reduce panic responses and overwhelming reactions, allowing for more self-reliance and confidence.

The ability to identify and eventually reconcile PTSD is in no way an easy journey. This is something I acknowledge as a survivor of PTSD following the sudden death of my 17-month-old daughter more than 20 years ago. The psychological and emotional pain you feel is real, and the path toward finding purpose in your pain is challenging. But it is possible to work through the barriers that get in the way of a peaceful, well-balanced life.

Perhaps you have felt lonely, isolated, misunderstood, and stuck. These are common responses and, as you begin this journey, you will discover that you aren't stuck—you're just struggling with the belief that you are isolated and don't know how to get better. A lack of skills to manage your symptoms makes it harder to get the support you need to feel better, think better, and calm your nervous system. By exploring and practicing the skills in this workbook, we will walk together, knowing that your pain is understood.

The supportive tools and exercises to deal with those intense emotions will help you learn to use DBT skills to care for yourself and allow others to care for you. The benefit of taking the first step is that your family, friends, and loved ones will hopefully follow your brave example because you are showing up for yourself. This workbook offers you skills, insight, and a new perspective on the complexities of trauma. Using the DBT strategies throughout will help you significantly minimize any distressing, intrusive thoughts and strong emotional reactions while you learn to cope and function better. As you courageously begin this journey toward personal wellness, explore each page with the awareness that you will learn not solely to survive but to thrive.

HOW TO USE THIS BOOK

This workbook can help you reconcile your PTSD symptoms, manage your intrusive thoughts, regulate strong emotions that have been difficult to identify and process, and cope with distress that is unmanageable. It's structured to be easy to use, interactive, and engaging. Specifically, it offers you a physically manageable text that's comfortable enough to carry with you whenever you need it. The workbook format gives you the space to write, respond to questions, revisit affirmations that resonate with you, and reflect on each chapter as you learn and develop new skills.

You may choose to use this book independently or with your therapist, or, if you are a medical professional or therapist, you can use this workbook with your clients. The goal is to learn how to feel supported and have the structure you need to create an effective journey to healing. As you learn DBT skills, you may find that you need additional space to write, reflect, or note down thoughts or questions about things that you need to revisit. Feel free to use a separate journal as a companion to this workbook if you need more room to write.

While there's no right or wrong way to use this workbook, it's important that you work consistently so that DBT skills become a fluid, natural response in your life. The structure and progression of the workbook will allow this to happen. You will find that your DBT skills build within each of the four modules and that the specific skills within the chapters complement those learned in previous chapters.

At the start of each chapter is an affirmation to set the intention for the chapter topic. This will allow your mind time to validate the challenging work you will do as you review the chapter overview. These affirmations allow your mind to prepare for the work with purpose, to decrease your anxiety and fears as you learn a new way to function, and to practice positive, self-affirming thoughts. Each skill is explained and connected with what you can expect as the chapter progresses. Each chapter is clearly identified by topic and includes exercises that you can practice as you become more proficient using DBT. At the conclusion of each chapter is a summary of what was presented, along with a list of key takeaway points so that you clearly understand what you learned and can celebrate your success.

An Important Safety Reminder

This workbook is intended to support people diagnosed with PTSD symptoms so they can find relief and learn the skills necessary to better manage the after-effects of trauma. If DBT has been recommended to you for diagnoses such as borderline personality disorder (BPD), bipolar disorder, or psychotic disorders, or if you have elevated levels of distress resulting in self-injurious behaviors, suicidal or homicidal ideation, or strong urges that are extremely difficult to regulate, it is strongly suggested that you use this book in conjunction with a licensed medical professional (your psychiatrist or family physician) along with a *licensed DBT-certified therapist*. This will ensure the appropriate level of guid-ance and support needed to gain the most benefit—it is always wise to ensure safety as a priority.

Understandably, it may be difficult to know when and if you need to work with professionals or a DBT-certified therapist. Here are a few statements that can help you make the choice that keeps you safe in this process:

- I am unable or unwilling to ensure that I can keep myself or others safe physically, psychologically, or emotionally.

- I am struggling with identifying what I am thinking or feeling.

- I have strong behavioral urges with harmful consequences.

- I have a history of self-injurious behavior.

- I have a history of inpatient, partial program, or intensive outpatient treatment.

- I am currently taking psychiatric medication that I consider challenging to take as prescribed.

- I am frequently unable or unwilling to use skills to reduce my vulnerabilities.

If any of the above items apply to you, it's wise to seek professional assis-tance or support to work through the therapeutic strategies presented in this workbook. If you struggle to find support, a variety of helpful information in the Resources section of this workbook can assist you with connecting with what you need to keep you safe while you do this work. Alternatively, you can consult your primary care physician, a trusted friend, or your insurance provider to find the support that you may need in order to ensure your safety.

The Importance of Working with a DBT-Certified Therapist

You may be wondering why it's important to work with a DBT-certified therapist as opposed to other mental health professionals, such as a psychiatrist or licensed professional counselor. The truth is that each helping professional offers something specific that's aimed at increasing your comfort and decreasing your upset. But what they focus on during your treatment may be vastly different than what you need, which often causes a disconnect between client and clinician during treatment.

For example, a licensed professional counselor (LPC) may focus on what is currently happening in your life, or your presenting symptoms, but they lack the clinical skills to help you cope with the underlying issues at the root of a problem that must be explored when struggling with a trauma history. For people with PTSD, an LPC may be helpful but is not the best choice to relieve the distress, work through past traumatic events, and teach the structured skills that DBT offers.

In contrast, a psychiatrist is a specialized medical doctor who focuses on managing physical symptoms and primarily prescribes medication in order to provide symptom relief. While this may be helpful when dealing with panic or irritability, because visits are typically brief and infrequent, they don't include psychotherapy to address past trauma. A DBT-certified psychotherapist is most helpful because they need specialized training with a highly qualified trainer—typically another DBT-certified therapist—to provide the specific skills to support people who have high levels of distress, a history of trauma, and a variety of psychological disorders that require this level of care. Because DBT is structured and consistent and includes a reliable set of modules tested over the course of decades, it has proven efficacy to stabilize trauma with long-term success. Therefore, finding a therapist who is qualified, is certified, and will ensure you are always moving forward and upward is an invaluable service to yourself.

CHAPTER 1

Understanding PTSD and DBT

*Although I have experienced pain, distress, and suffering
throughout my life—whether witnessed or felt—I have survived
it all and am choosing a new path.*

In this section, you'll develop a general understanding of posttraumatic stress disorder (PTSD) and dialectical behavior therapy (DBT). We'll begin with defining what PTSD is, how it differs from other types of traumatic experiences, and how it presents in our behavioral responses. We will then explore avoidance, dissociation, self-harm, and suicidal behavior, and identify how long symptoms may last and the long-term effects if PTSD is left untreated. To help you understand how and why PTSD happens, this chapter introduces the benefits and helpful aspects of trauma responses and how they may have helped you in your life. Before we move into DBT, you'll do a self-assessment that will help you evaluate your trauma and PTSD symptoms.

We'll then proceed with understanding what DBT is, how it differs from other approaches, and why it is helpful with PTSD. You will learn the four core modules of DBT and how they relate and work together. You will also learn how DBT was developed and how it can be useful to you as you find your way to an extraordinary new way of living.

What Is PTSD?

In this section, we will define what PTSD is and what causes it. We'll look at four categories used when diagnosing the PTSD symptoms that you may have been experiencing. You'll be able to do a self-assessment for behavior, thought processes, emotional responses, and physical symptoms to help identify issues of concern in these four categories.

Although some people who have experienced traumatic events seem to resolve the symptoms in a short time and eventually thrive, far more experience residual effects of traumatic events due to prior diagnoses of anxiety or depressive disorders. Initial symptoms may include decreased focus, inability to sleep (insomnia), irritability, agitation, and an overall sense of imminent threat or harm immediately following the onset of the traumatic event.

The type of trauma an individual experiences is an important factor in determining whether the trauma may have long-term symptoms that do not immediately resolve. Another factor to consider is whether the trauma is repeated or prolonged, such as with veterans who have repeated tours of duty. For civilians, physical or sexual abuse may also present PTSD symptoms due to the impact and repetition of this type of trauma. Increasing numbers of people have experienced chronic, prolonged trauma and report having symptoms similar to those who have served in the military.

Considering the level of impact and the lasting effects on people who responded to or witnessed the events may help in understanding the difference between stressful events and posttraumatic stress. In the next section, we will break down the most harmful behavioral symptoms.

How Trauma Manifests as Behaviors

Some of the more significant issues with trauma are the strong behavioral responses that result from the distress from prior traumatic events or during a current, chronic, or recurring traumatic event. Unresolved posttraumatic stress increases the risk of self-harm, recurrent suicidal ideation, and suicide attempts to manage the distress. This is due to a person's lack of knowledge of how to reduce the physical alarm to the nervous system when the body intensely floods itself with adrenaline to prepare for the possibility of a new or recurring threat. Repeated overload of the senses from repeated traumatic events accumulates and increases the likelihood that an individual with PTSD will make multiple suicide attempts.

Additional issues with unresolved trauma include vulnerability to other mental health issues, recurring trauma, incarceration, isolation, and strained relationships. The use and misuse of illegal substances, or the use of substances in excess to avoid feeling or to feel better, is a harmful behavioral response to manage distress. When people have difficulty managing negative thoughts related to those events, it often also results in hypervigilance, moodiness, insomnia, poor concentration, and aggressive, reactive responses toward others. Let's look further at three specific behavioral responses related to PTSD.

AVOIDANCE

Avoidance is an effort to control visual memories and emotions that are similar to a traumatic event or to control the feeling experienced during a traumatic event. A person may resort to avoiding people, places, things, and scenarios that activate the senses related to the event. The primary issue with having a PTSD diagnosis is that the intrusive thoughts and feelings related to traumatic events are random, so if someone can achieve a sense of control through avoidance, it feels like a way to stave off dissociation, which we explore in the next section. The intention of avoidance is to avoid the feeling of distress, thereby calming and regulating the central nervous system, which decreases panic attacks. But it increases the possibility that a person will struggle with depressive episodes and moodiness due to the isolation and inability to connect with their supports, since they may be avoiding people as well as the memories, emotions, or things that caused the trauma.

DISSOCIATION

Dissociation is a behavioral response that happens when avoidance is unsuccessful. Flashbacks, also known as dissociative reactions, make it feel like the traumatic event is occurring in the present. This level of distress can result in loss of time or orientation, and a person may feel separated from their surroundings, people, or themselves. There are two types of dissociation—depersonalization and derealization—and both are the body's attempt to protect itself from the sense of recurring threat.

Depersonalization is the out-of-body experience that many people report when having a sense of being detached from their own identity. While they are able to function in a seemingly normal way, this PTSD symptom causes their mind to feel disconnected from the present reality, as if they're watching it happen rather than experiencing it. Derealization differs in that it makes you feel like you are disconnected from the world and people around you—almost like you are cut off from reality. In a similar way to depersonalization, derealization disconnects the individual from their environment in order to not activate a distress response.

Although dissociation may decrease the sense of threat and fear, it increases detachment from interpersonal relationships and, similar to avoidance, inability to connect with friends, family, and the necessary professional support to manage trauma using skills and understanding from loved ones.

SELF-HARM OR SUICIDE

The most concerning of the behavioral responses to PTSD are self-harm or the consideration of suicide. Although it may be difficult for family or other supporting people to understand, for people who have recurrent flashbacks, distressing dreams, and sensory overload, these behaviors are an effort to stop what seems to never end. Self-harm or self-injurious behavior (SIB) is a method people use to dull the pain and intensity of what they are feeling in their bodies or in the physical environment. It has also been described as a way to make themselves feel something to be more connected with others and the environment. Self-harm differs from suicidality, which is the risk of suicide by thought or intention and is associated with frequent episodes of traumatic responses when the distress feels unbearable and there is a sense of hopelessness.

Self-harm is never an effective solution, as it cannot provide long-term relief for a person with PTSD. The act of suicide is equally ineffective, because it traumatizes those who surround the person who has died by suicide, leaving more people living with residual trauma. Suicide may seem like a good solution to someone experiencing extreme distress, but it is never the best way to find relief. This book can help you deal with distressing symptoms, and the Resources section (see page 158) includes additional places to find support in handling suicidal thoughts.

PTSD Self-Evaluation

Below are common PTSD symptoms (adapted from the *DSM-V*) that you may be experiencing related to a traumatic event. Check the box of the symptoms that apply to you.

☐ I experienced, witnessed, or learned of a traumatic event.

☐ I have difficulty forgetting the event.

☐ I avoid things related to the event.

☐ I think negative thoughts about a variety of things related to the event.

☐ I have had difficulty concentrating following the event.

☐ I struggle with my level of functioning at work, school, etc. since the event.

☐ I have been told, or I sense, that I have become moodier following the event.

☐ I have had nightmares and flashbacks of the event.

☐ I have had trouble sleeping (feeling restless when trying to sleep) since the event.

☐ I feel distant, detached, or in a dream state since the event.

If you checked one or two items: You may be experiencing signs of PTSD.

If you checked three or four items: It is likely that you may be experiencing signs of PTSD.

If you checked five or more items: You can be certain that you are experiencing signs of PTSD.

Only a qualified clinician can offer a definitive diagnosis, but this is a good start to learn which symptoms are problematic and related to PTSD.

The Core Principles of DBT

Dialectical behavior therapy (DBT) is an empirically proven, effective treatment for people who have difficulty managing intense emotions and interpersonal relationships. Initially developed by Dr. Marsha Linehan, DBT counteracts the tendency to think, feel, and behave in extremes. It helps people achieve increased levels of self-regulation and a stronger sense of control in challenging and difficult situations. Dr. Linehan developed DBT for people diagnosed with borderline personality disorder who were experiencing high-risk, harmful behaviors. She had success with this new perspective using a dialectical approach. Many clients have thought of a dialectic as a way of speaking (the word *dialectic* is often confused with the word *dialect*). Honestly, it is a shift toward a new, more balanced way of communicating and is a language of its own. To have a dialectical approach is to offer and consider a gradient ranging between the "all" or "nothing" extremes of thought. The approach toward a dialectic requires someone to know how to effectively use DBT skills, especially when life is distressing and unsafe or when traumatic events occur.

DBT comprises a variety of skills within four modules developed to work collectively and supportively. For example, the emotion regulation skills support the interpersonal effectiveness skills when an individual needs to express what is happening emotionally with increased clarity and a sense of calm. We will look at each skill's primary use and further instruct how to apply these skills to situations related to PTSD and other co-occurring mental health diagnoses. Let's explore each module individually and see how they all work together.

Mindfulness

Mindfulness is a foundational DBT skill that makes it easier to know how to calmly approach specific situations and life in general. The objective is to be present during an experience so that you can feel grounded when you're upset or under stress. It teaches a new way of functioning by living in a present state of awareness, focusing on the gift of being a centered, well-balanced human *being*, not solely a human *doing*. Mindfulness helps people with PTSD manage symptoms using sensory awareness, body awareness through progressive muscle relaxation, and regulated breathing to calm the body. This skill focuses on awareness and life satisfaction through a shift in the mind, allowing for more problem-solving in the moment of a crisis or traumatic event when our choices seem limited. It relies on being mindful and increasingly aware of our stress or distress levels and what skill is working so the dialectical shift can be made quickly. Mindfulness is the first of the four DBT modules you will learn, as it allows increased understanding of the three states of mind that will be explained in chapter 2.

Distress Tolerance

With an understanding of PTSD, we can explore what distress is and learn the DBT skill that helps remedy it. While many of us have a "typical" response to upset, which resolves in a regressive manner, other people have strong, high-impact waves of upset that feel overwhelming and out of control. It is as if they are drowning in emotions and thoughts with no way to swim through them and get back to a safe shore. The stress of this experience is isolating and fearful, and the water from the wave blocks out any potential help.

Distress tolerance offers the life raft to pull you to shore so you can connect with the help you may be unable to hear during a time of feeling emotionally overwhelmed, panicky, or ruminating about thoughts that lead to those emotional states. There will be a more in-depth explanation in the chapters related to distress tolerance and emotion regulation. For people with PTSD, distress tolerance skills can reduce flashbacks and mood swings and foster balanced communication.

Emotion Regulation

Understanding distress tolerance to manage the PTSD symptoms helps you learn about emotion regulation. To better understand what emotional dysregulation is, think back to the time when you were a small child, when you first learned how to express feelings. Over time, you learned to control and regulate your emotions and tolerated more complicated feelings as you developed. As we grow, we learn that there are unsafe situations and experiences, and in those moments that challenge the safety we once knew, some people struggle to reconcile this new level of awareness. For people with PTSD, this results in maladaptive behaviors because they don't have the ability to regulate strong emotions. Emotion regulation offers a variety of solutions and clarity, resulting in increased control and understanding of moments of distress, with less panic and reactivity and minimal unsafe maladaptive responses.

Interpersonal Effectiveness

The final module focuses on the skills required to strengthen existing relation-ships and to feel a sense of self-worth as you learn how to develop healthier, more supportive relationships and interactions. DBT skills in this module teach strategies for asking others to consider and listen to your needs and wants. This helps you increase well-balanced communication, resolve conflicts, identify and stay true to your values, offer and give respect, and work toward connecting during moments of isolation, depression, and despair. As the mindfulness skill works toward being present, interpersonal effectiveness allows mindfulness to be the support within interactions and when communicating with others.

As distress tolerance works to hold back the fear response when you have the urge to avoid difficult conversations or to disconnect through dissociation, mindfulness brings someone with PTSD to the present long enough to recognize the emotion. They can then use interpersonal effectiveness to ask for support or what is needed in that moment to regulate the distress. DBT skills create the opportunity to better gain control by being able to progressively learn how to minimize avoidance, regulate emotions, and be mindful of self and others while integrating with the other three DBT modules as the foundation for a well-balanced and enjoyable life.

Key Takeaways

Congratulations! You now have a foundation for the rest of the workbook and have developed an overall understanding of PTSD and the contributing factors that cause a person to experience it. Here are the key things you have learned from this chapter:

- You know what PTSD is, what causes it, and how it relates to traumatic events.

- You learned behavioral, emotional, psychological, and physical responses relative to PTSD and traumatic events.

- From your self-evaluation, you were able to reflect on your own symptoms and better understand where you may be struggling.

- You learned about the development of DBT and its four modules: mindfulness, distress tolerance, emotion regulation, and interpersonal effectiveness.

- You now have a clearer understanding of how trauma affects thoughts, emotions, actions, and the body.

- You confidently understand the intention of this workbook and why it was created to support your journey to wellness.

CHAPTER 2

DBT Module: Mindfulness

I have a level of awareness that teaches me to live each day with intention. I am prepared to use mindfulness skills to add stability to my life.

In this section of the workbook, you'll gain a more specific understanding of the core principles of DBT. Each of the following four chapters begins with a more detailed overview of each of the four primary DBT skills you learned from chapter 1. Throughout each module, you'll have an opportunity to put the skills into practice. These exercises are designed to help you relate to real-life scenarios and experiences you may have had. They focus on specific skill use, self-evaluation, and how each skill targets symptoms to help with PTSD.

First, you'll learn about mindfulness and the specific DBT skills that are in the Mindfulness Module. We'll further explore the benefits of mindfulness, including learning the language of DBT with skill sets such as WHAT and HOW. Finally, you will learn the benefit of making space and setting a routine. By the end of this chapter, you will significantly increase your skill set and, most important, be able to regulate problematic PTSD symptoms.

What Is Mindfulness?

The topic of mindfulness is frequently misunderstood. Mindfulness skills are the foundation of DBT, and they're the first DBT skills introduced when working with a DBT-certified therapist. This includes learning the three states of mind that enable you to gain better control over your thoughts and emotions.

For people with PTSD, core mindfulness skills help create more opportunities to regain control of a mind that may become easily emotionally dysregulated, have strong negative thoughts associated with past traumatic events, and be highly vulnerable to distress when experiencing sensory overload. Mindfulness skills allow those with PTSD to pay attention to what the mind is focusing on and the time that is used focusing on things. By taking the time to learn about yourself in this way, you can increase your understanding of why you make certain choices and how you think and feel about your thoughts, feelings, and experiences. Mindfulness increases the control of how and when to focus attention on experiences with the objective of living mindfully.

As discussed in the previous chapter, mindfulness is an integral foundation skill that gives you the support you need to build on the skills to come. So, it is important to work consistently and with a schedule. Within this chapter, you will learn the great benefit of setting a routine, and using this workbook with a schedule is an opportunity to begin using that skill.

As we explore the benefits of mindfulness, you will work on an exercise that will allow you to self-evaluate how you may be coping in a "mindless" way. The chapter will then explore the three states of mind as we discover the rationale of mindfulness being used to manage PTSD. Practicing at a steady pace will give you the ability to add to your knowledge at each skill level.

The Benefits of Mindfulness for PTSD

Because of the level of distress and strong responses associated with PTSD, mindfulness can be a great benefit. For symptoms such as flashbacks and coping skills such as dissociation, mindfulness allows for a refocusing of attention and has significant advantages. For example, using mindfulness supports better symptom management and increases an understanding of what is happening in a present moment. Because PTSD symptoms make staying in the present very difficult due to intrusive visuals within the mind, it often feels like a traumatic event from the past is happening in the present. With the use of mindfulness skills, those symptoms can be greatly reduced, thereby increasing distress tolerance by using DBT skills in times of emotional and psychological distress.

Another use of mindfulness is the ability to regulate a distressed, overwhelmingly emotional mind. Because the rational mind works to balance the emotions and to regulate toward a wise mind, the result may be a decrease in distress. By focusing on one thing at a time, you can minimize fear-based thoughts that were once overwhelming. We will explore emotional mind, rational mind, and wise mind in the next section. Additional mindfulness strategies include learning to understand without judgment to support effective decision-making during stressful or difficult moments. These are a few examples of the benefits you will learn as you work through the exercises and build competency and proficiency with each skill. Now, let's take a look at your level of mindfulness or "mindlessness" in the following self-evaluation.

Evaluating "Mindless" Coping Strategies

The list below contains common "mindless" ways to cope with stress and distress. Check the symptoms that apply to you to identify the level of mindlessness you are experiencing.

☐ I am a multitasker, especially when I am under stress.

☐ I panic when I make mistakes.

☐ I struggle with forgiving others for mistakes.

☐ My thoughts about tasks that are unfinished (e.g., chores, projects) "consume" me.

☐ I have difficulty concentrating even when I plan to relax or take a vacation.

☐ My focus is easily distracted when my emotions are overwhelming.

☐ I am often seen as moody or irritable when things don't go my way.

☐ I can't sleep until my home is completely clean or kept the way I like it.

☐ I don't accept myself as I am most days.

☐ I am unable to sit quietly with my thoughts and feelings for more than five minutes at a time.

If you checked one to three items: You have things to work on, and you've already started, so celebrate that.

If you checked four to six items: You have received this workbook in time to eliminate mindlessness once and for all.

If you checked seven to ten items: You are definitely living mindlessly, yet you have chosen mindfulness to be better and keep working at it.

Understanding the Three States of Mind

DBT explores three states of mind: rational, emotional, and wise. In rational mind, we think of facts and what we believe. In emotional mind, we think based on our emotional state and how we feel. The issue with PTSD and functioning from either of these states of mind is that we negate the other state and are guided by our thoughts or feelings due to the sense of threat. As we begin examining ourselves through a DBT perspective, we work to balance both extremes to achieve wise mind. Although most of us tend to be either thinking or feeling people, we need new knowledge to achieve wise mind. Mindfulness skills are the foundation of this.

Mindfulness includes WHAT skills, which focus on learning to be an observer of self and others, including the environment and what occurs outside of yourself. WHAT skills teach us to put words on what we're experiencing and then decide whether we participate. WHAT skills include attending to your emotions, thoughts, and feelings, as well as what you think about how you feel. This also includes your experiences and people. What we think and how we feel about ourselves and others allow us to make wise mind decisions about how we act and respond. To support the WHAT are complementary skills referred to as HOW. How we approach our emotions and thoughts is integral to achieving emotional and psychological balance as we begin making wise mind decisions.

Exploring Your Own Mind

What you tell yourself is an extremely important part of recovering from PTSD. You may have noticed when using the DBT skills you've learned so far that what you say to yourself is important and so is what you feel and think about your world. Having PTSD symptoms challenges your ability to think in a balanced way, leading to negative thoughts, feelings, and behaviors resulting in distorted beliefs and perceptions. As you continue to learn how to become more aware while exploring the three states of mind, you will better understand what you think and feel. Using the skill of exploring your own mind allows you to focus on the present moment when you are saying things to yourself, perhaps silently when no one else can hear you. For those with PTSD, finding the source of negative self-talk and the solution to fight it allows for healthier functioning using mindfulness.

Exploring Your Mind with Mindful Solutions

Below is a list of common negative self-talk words and phrases that you may use in a "mindless" way. See if you can match the list with the mindful solution. The answers to this exercise are in the back of the workbook (see page 164).

"Mindless" Thoughts and Phrases (Column I)	Match the letter from Column I with the number in Column II	Mindful Solutions to Understand What I'm Actually Saying and Doing (Column II)
a. I can't		1. I should focus on what I am able and willing to do.
b. It's hard		2. I need time to discover the why since I may already know.
c. But . . .		3. I feel regret and remorse.
d. You don't understand		4. I don't know how and when to change or I'm scared to change.
e. I'll always be this way		5. I don't know if I have the ability.
f. Nobody gets me		6. I haven't found a person(s) that gets me.
g. I'll try		7. I'm afraid to let you in and am unsure that if I do you will understand me.
h. Should, would, and could		8. Things are difficult or challenging/hard, and I have a barrier to protect myself.
i. Good/bad or Right/wrong		9. I'm stuck in a negative mindset, so I'm going to negate whatever you say.
j. Why?		10. I don't feel safe and am having PTSD symptoms.

Emotional Mind

Now let's explore the emotional mind, which is the quality of how you feel about someone, something, or an experience. When we're in emotional mind, we express, and often behave, according to what we feel about a situation. We often don't consider what we think about a situation and instead focus on what we feel or what we think we're feeling. Our decision-making is frequently reactive and impulsive, with little regard for the potential negative consequences that result from emotional choices.

As we've learned in the previous chapter, for people with PTSD, significant levels of emotional distress create a vulnerability to think from emotional mind. This reduces the ability to make well-balanced and safe choices. As a consequence, there may be occurrences of traumatization and an inability to withstand distress. The next exercise will help you get a better understanding of emotional mind.

Minding My Emotional Mind

For this exercise, focus on understanding how your emotions express themselves like thoughts. Listed below are commonly experienced emotions:

afraid	empathic	hopeful	nervous	suspicious
angry	empty	hopeless	proud	terrified
annoyed	energetic	horrified	regretful	thrilled
anxious	enraged	hurt	relieved	tIred
bored	excited	hysterical	respected	unappreciated
cautious	exhausted	irritated	sad	unsure
confident	frightened	jealous	satisfied	upset
content	frustrated	joyful	scared	worried
curious	guilty	lonely	shy	worthless
depressed	happy	loved	surprised	worthy

Circle the 10 emotions that you experience most frequently. From those 10, select 1 for this exercise. You may choose your most intense emotion or something easier to work on for now. The goal of this exercise is to break down your emotions and identify your emotional mind that speaks thoughts based on emotions.

My exploration emotion is: ....

Experiences I have had when I feel this emotion:

....

....

....

Thinking about this emotion, I feel these bodily sensations:

....

....

....

What I have done when I feel this emotion:

....

....

....

Thoughts I have when I experience this emotion:

....

....

....

What I have learned from exploring this emotion:

....

....

....

Rational Mind

Now let's learn about the rational mind so we can better understand what we need to work with in order to find our way to wise mind. The rational mind, which is often referred to as *the reasonable mind* or *the logical mind*, is when we approach a situation based on facts, data, intellect, and what we focus on in our minds.

This state of mind fails to consider how we feel about our experiences, similar to how the emotional mind fails to consider the facts concerning a situation. You can see that the rational mind can lead to additional issues, especially for people with PTSD, who may have negative thoughts and beliefs due to the experiences related to traumatic events. Consequences may include being more rigid with thought and having difficulty negotiating relationships and needs. It can lead to all-or-nothing thinking and makes it difficult to relate to others since we are not solely thoughts and beliefs—we also have feelings that must be considered.

Checking the Facts of My Rational Mind

Write three common thoughts you have about your life, experiences, people, or any other category of your life. You may also write three thoughts you have about yourself.

1. ....
....

2. ....
....

3. ....
....

Now focus on the first thought and take a moment to reflect on the source of the thought based on facts. Then, do the same for each of the other thoughts.

1. The source of this thought is ....
....
....

2. The source of this thought is ....
....
....

3. The source of this thought is ....
....
....

continued

continued from page 21

After you've identified the sources, reflect on the effects these thoughts have had on how you think about life and how you function. Use the space below to bring all three thoughts and the facts related to those thoughts together into a paragraph. Take the time to think about changes you may want to make with how you think.

_____

_____

_____

_____

_____

_____

_____

_____

_____

_____

_____

_____

_____

_____

_____

_____

_____

_____

Wise Mind

To achieve wise mind is to find the dialectical balance between emotional mind and rational mind. We achieve this when we're able to recognize and respect what we feel emotionally while considering what we think and feel based on facts. When experiencing upsetting emotions about traumatic events such as fear, using wise mind allows us to consider the facts about what is happening in the present moment. You can work through these emotional experiences to understand that you are safe in the present moment.

When in wise mind, we validate the experiences from both an emotional and rational mind. This allows for integration of the two states of mind, leading to effective decision-making and less distressful experiences. The wise mind creates a sense of balance between the two extremes that allows us to function in a healthier way. Now that we understand the three states of mind, let's reinforce everything that you've just learned.

A State of Wisdom

Below are 10 statements using the three states of mind you just learned. Identify whether the state of mind related to each example is the emotional, rational, or wise mind. Answers can be found in the back of this workbook (see page 164).

a. I can't do it, regardless of what you say! ....

b. I think I can't finish my assignment, and I believe I may be overtired.

....

c. I am willing to think before I respond to a request. ....

d. Therapy doesn't work, so I'll just cancel all my sessions. ....

e. I feel overwhelmed and need take a break. ....

f. I appreciate my life in spite of the trauma I have experienced.

....

g. I know you think you know what's best for me, but I know myself better.

....

h. I don't know what I'm feeling, so stop asking me. ....

i. Leave me alone so I can process my thoughts and feelings.

....

j. I've used DBT in the past, and it brought out feelings I'm not willing to explore.

....

Using Mindfulness Skills for PTSD

Mindfulness skills create a foundation to find better ways to live and have positive experiences. They give you improved control of your mind, increasing your ability to focus and concentrate on things that may have once had control over you. Functioning this way adds to your ability to be intentional and aware, creating a more balanced shift in the way you see things. It allows you to be more connected, be less judgmental, and live in the present. Because people with a trauma history tend to isolate and distort thoughts, it's beneficial to learn mindfulness skills to better cope with symptoms.

People struggling with PTSD often create negative core beliefs based on their experiences and focus on past experiences to keep safe. These assumptions can further distort beliefs about the future based on upsetting recollections from the past. With PTSD, there is difficulty understanding how to function in a world that feels unsafe, which makes it hard to know how to function in general and how to relate to others interpersonally. As recurring traumatic events continue to challenge how we respond, it can be difficult to find solutions when in distress. By using mindfulness skills, we begin to retrain the brain with new knowledge to heal from prior traumatic events and to heal from the traumatic stress associated with PTSD. As we move through this chapter, you'll learn the benefit of using foundation skills such as observation, description, and participation—also known as WHAT skills. You will also learn HOW skills, which include focusing on one thing at a time functionally and in a nonjudgmental way, and doing what works. With mindfulness skills, we seek to reduce PTSD reactive stress responses and allow for processing of present and repressed trauma memories to minimize avoidance, dissociation, self-harm, and suicidality.

WHAT Skills

WHAT skills are what you need to achieve wise mind. This skill set includes observation, description, and participation. These skills give us the opportunity to enter into an experience like a detective by noticing an experience without connecting to it. This is key to observation.

The observation part of the WHAT skill considers things that happen within yourself and also in your environment. For those struggling with PTSD, this increases the ability to understand what's being felt in the body and occurring with the senses, as it relates to the experience being observed.

The second WHAT skill is description. To describe is to put words and language on those observations by assisting the mind to make sense of what is occurring. Description begins the processing of information you have witnessed, which helps with how to proceed with what to do next.

The skill that supports this process is participation, the last of the WHAT skills. As observation and description increase your awareness, participation allows you to choose to be a part of what is being observed.

OBSERVATION

Observation helps you gain better control of your mind, allowing you to gather information and learn how to respond to what you're detecting. Sight, sound, smell, taste, and touch trigger the signals to activate observation during an experience. With PTSD, this skill increases how the mind responds to those signals.

DESCRIPTION

Description focuses on putting words and language to an experience. As you observe, it's equally important to be able to say to yourself, or a trusted support person, what is happening as you use your senses. With PTSD, this creates improved communication and understanding of self to manage symptoms.

PARTICIPATION

Participation gives the opportunity to act and enter into experiences and focus on action in exchange for reaction. The key to this skill is to connect and be part of, not consumed by, an experience. Trusting your intuition using wise mind allows those with PTSD to gently enter and depart from situations, experiences, and interactions.

Observing the Senses

In this scenario, we will explore how to understand an observation that is being described. Read the scenario for Asia, who has been diagnosed with PTSD. Use wise mind to help understand this experience. The answer to this scenario is in the back of the workbook (see page 164).

> *Asia is a college senior with a close group of friends who are trustworthy and have been helpful following an assault on Asia during a party when she was a freshman. Asia's roommate informs her that Asia seems to be fighting in her sleep, is growling, and sounds like she is grinding her teeth while yelling, "Don't touch me!" What might Asia be observing in her mind?*

The Supportive WHAT Detective

Now let's test your WHAT skills to determine whether what is described is an opportunity to participate in the experience. Then identify the reason why it is helpful or harmful. Read the scenario for Lynne, who has been diagnosed with PTSD. Use wise mind to help understand this experience. The answer to this scenario is in the back of the workbook (see page 164).

> Lynne has returned to work after a car accident that totaled her car. Lynne was able to survive the accident with minimal physical injuries, but she has poor sleep and stomach pain and has been working with a therapist for six weeks since the accident. Lynne is afraid to return to work and does not want to participate in a phone call with her boss with a return-to-work plan. Is it helpful or harmful for Lynne to participate with her boss to discuss the plan? What is the reason for your choice?

HOW Skills

HOW skills are how you apply and use the WHAT skills you've just learned as you work toward wise mind. The HOW skills include nonjudgmentally, one-mindfully, and effectively. While what we do helps us to become aware, how we process that information is equally important. HOW skills allow us to create a mental picture and notice experiences without labeling. Focusing on one thing at a time when observing increases your ability to gather more information and to effectively process before deciding to participate in experiences.

These three HOW skills, along with the WHAT skills, create the foundation for wise mind decisions. For example, during an observation of an event, I am using one-mindfully to focus on one thing at a time. I am checking in with myself and with my environment. As I describe in nonjudgmental language (within my mind), I am processing information more effectively. I am then able to choose whether I participate in this event or participate in something different that is more effective. When considering the distress related to PTSD, the combination of HOW and WHAT skills offers a strategy to prevent judgmental, negative thoughts and poor decisions.

NONJUDGMENTALLY

The willingness to think nonjudgmentally requires you to focus on facts to minimize distorting information. Like a detective, focus on information without extremes. Use *who*, *what*, *where*, and *when* to describe observed experiences. Although you may have times when you judge, it's important to be willing to shift to nonjudgment.

ONE-MINDFULLY

One-mindfully increases the ability to focus on one thing at a time with complete attention. While we struggle with daily distractions, this skill allows you to gently notice and let go of those distractions. The key to one-mindfulness is to refocus by offering loving kindness to yourself as you work toward present-moment awareness.

EFFECTIVELY

Effectively is how to do what works. The key to functioning effectively is to consider the context of a situation, allowing for easy acceptance of what is happening. Along with willingness, using effectiveness while remaining nonjudgmental helps avoid extremes in thought and emotions, increasing the ability to make wise mind decisions.

Nonjudgmental Language

This exercise is to test your ability to identify nonjudgmental language. Circle either JUDGMENTAL or NONJUDGMENTAL based on each statement listed below.

1.	That was the dumbest thing you've done so far.	JUDGMENTAL	NONJUDGMENTAL
2.	I hate my life.	JUDGMENTAL	NONJUDGMENTAL
3.	I understand my struggles.	JUDGMENTAL	NONJUDGMENTAL
4.	I can tolerate our differences.	JUDGMENTAL	NONJUDGMENTAL
5.	I'm aware that life is challenging, but I'm committed to doing what it takes to feel better.	JUDGMENTAL	NONJUDGMENTAL
6.	I understand my struggles, but it's so hard to use skills.	JUDGMENTAL	NONJUDGMENTAL
7.	I can't deal with my emotions right now.	JUDGMENTAL	NONJUDGMENTAL
8.	You don't understand my suffering or my pain.	JUDGMENTAL	NONJUDGMENTAL
9.	Leave me alone!	JUDGMENTAL	NONJUDGMENTAL
10.	I need time to process, so please give me space.	JUDGMENTAL	NONJUDGMENTAL

The answer key is located in the back of this workbook (see page 164).

Score = _____

Hopefully you were able to identify the correct responses and understand that judgmental language can be subtle. The next exercise will help you practice being nonjudgmental.

Practicing a Nonjudgmental Stance

During the next week, complete the following chart identifying when you have used judgmental language. Then take a stance and correct using nonjudgmental language. Do your best and practice, practice, practice.

MY NONJUDGMENTAL PRACTICE LOG

Day of the Week	My Judgmental Language	My Nonjudgmental Stance
Sunday		
Monday		
Tuesday		
Wednesday		
Thursday		
Friday		
Saturday		

Additional Mindfulness Skills for PTSD

Up to this point, you've learned the foundational skills within the DBT mindfulness module. But there are other skills that create the consistency and safety to control what comes into the mind and what stays out. In this section, we will create the structure to support what you now know. We need to make the space for your safety and establish a routine to stay focused while setting goals. By using these supplementary mindfulness supports, you will develop a sense of security to practice wise mind.

As you find spaces that are physically, emotionally, and psychologically safe, you will reduce distress responses and enhance your ability to process them quickly. When you're able to manage symptoms with or without support, these safe spaces encourage the use of your mindfulness skills for thought processing and emotional exploration. This increases your ability to manage life better. A routine provides a structured sense of expectation that furthers consistent skill use while working through distressing experiences. By participating in this way, you will be reducing avoidance and establishing a balanced way of living. As we progress through this chapter, you'll learn the benefit of how these two skills are used and how they can be helpful for managing PTSD symptoms.

Making Space

As you continue to understand the difficulties of managing PTSD and ensuring safety, it's extremely important to find space to work through distress. The idea of making space may include finding safe physical space such as a room within your home or taking a warm bath to safely explore sensory skills. Other physical spaces may be outside the home. For some people, it may include being in nature, which is an example of an open space where you can meditate and create a sense of calm in a safe environment.

Another example may include allowing yourself the mental space to use the skills that you've learned so far. Frequently, we are consumed with thoughts and lists of things that we need to do each day. Taking time to unpack the mental tasks of each day grants you the psychological space to integrate DBT skills into your daily life. It's also important to consider emotional space. As we work through emotional issues such as resentment, anger, panic, or other strong emotions, giving yourself compassion to create safety for yourself is essential.

Finding My Physical Safe Space

We discussed the need for a physical safe space to process your thoughts and feelings. In the following exercise, you will identify your safe spaces.

1. On the lines listed below, identify your physical safe spaces.

    _____

    _____

    _____

    _____

    _____

2. Now explain why and how these safe spaces will help you.

    _____

    _____

    _____

    _____

    _____

Finding My Psychological and Emotional Safe Space

Now that you've identified your physical safe spaces, we need to work on how to keep your mind and emotions safe. These spaces may be the same as the previous exercise, but challenge yourself to find different spaces to add to your list. Mental safe spaces don't necessarily need to be tied to a physical location—for example, they could involve a calming activity or a mental picture of an imagined location.

1. On the lines listed below, identify your psychological and emotional safe spaces.

_____

_____

_____

_____

_____

2. Now explain why and how these safe spaces will help you.

_____

_____

_____

_____

_____

Setting a Routine

Along with making space, it's equally important to set the routine to support that space. But a routine requires commitment and consistency to be effective. The goal of creating and adhering to a routine is to provide structure and stability while preparing for expectation. For people with PTSD, a structured routine fosters a sense of control and prepares the mental space to do these tasks. Sticking with a routine also helps our bodies know when it's time to wake and to sleep and provides increased functioning to process thoughts and emotions when resting and sleeping.

Setting and adhering to your routine helps you offer compassion and respect for yourself, creating new and possibly hidden opportunities to relax. It also makes the time to connect with those you care about and to structure your self-care throughout the day. A routine in combination with space and your new skills will get you on the path toward living a more mindful and intentional life.

As you go about setting a routine in the following exercises, feel free to purchase a special calendar or be creative and use poster board to see your routine on your wall. You can also put your calendar in your smartphone so you can set reminders. Use emojis or other things that help you stay on track.

How Do I Start My Routine?

A routine creates structure to lock in your skill use and keep you safe. Give your-self one day to work on each item on this list to get you thinking, then we'll put it together in the next exercise.

1. **Find the What**
    What do you want? To find time to use your DBT skills or to use your safe space time to reflect? Make a list of what is a priority at this moment.

2. **Small and Achievable Goals**
    If your goals are too big, you're probably overdoing things and not being mindful. Instead, break each large goal into smaller goals. If your overall goal is to meditate each day, start with five minutes a day to build your commitment.

3. **Timing Is Everything**
    Learning whether you are more efficient in the morning or at night is important to your timing. Function when you are at your best to keep your commitment and motivation consistent.

4. **Do a Needs Assessment**
    Make sure you have what you need to be successful. For example, if the plan is to call a friend once per week, be sure your phone is charged and you have scheduled time for the call.

5. **Lighten Up**
    If setting a routine feels stressful, find support using the skills from this workbook or talking with someone you care about who may be working on the same goals. This can help you have fun.

6. **Progress and Self-Evaluation**
    Create a visual of your progress, such as a calendar that you can color code as you complete daily tasks.

7. **Rewards and Reinforcement**
    When you get that routine steady, check in each week and identify the fun reward for doing your best. For example, if the goal was to take a 15-minute bath each week, reward yourself with aromatherapy bath salts.

Putting the Pieces Together

Now that you know the steps needed to establish a routine, let's see an example of what it looks like on a calendar:

Goal 1: Spend more time with family, friends, and pet
Goal 2: Ask for help with chores, improve mood with fitness
Priorities: Health, skill use, improving relationships, self-care, and me time
Reward: New walking shoes for the park

	Sun	Mon	Tues	Wed	Thur	Fri	Sat
6 am	Sleep late day	Make breakfast and exercise	Make breakfast	Make breakfast and exercise	Make breakfast	Make breakfast and exercise	Mindful dog walk
8 am	Mindful walk with family	Work	Work	Work	Work	Work	Start laundry
10 am	Family brunch	15 min break/ work	15 min break/ work	15 min break/ work	15 min break/ work	15 min break/ work	Brunch with friends
12 pm	Movies with family	Lunch with coworker	Lunch alone	Lunch with coworker	Lunch alone	Lunch with coworker	Chores
2 pm	Self-care Sunday	15-minute break	15-minute break	15-minute break	15-minute break	15-minute break	Chores
4 pm	Self-care Sunday	Shopping	Exercise class	Creative time	Exercise class	Fun activity	Break
6 pm	Dinner with family	Dinner with family	Dinner with family	Dinner with family	Dinner with family	Dinner with family	Dinner with my partner
8 pm	Read my workbook	Read my workbook	Read my workbook	Read my workbook	Read my workbook	Read my workbook	Read my workbook
10 pm	Meditate	Meditate	Meditate	Meditate	Meditate	Meditate	Meditate

Key Takeaways

We explored quite a bit in this chapter—keep up the great work! Here are the key things you have learned:

- You know the entire set of DBT foundational skills and understand the concept of mindfulness and how it helps with PTSD.

- You identified your "mindless" coping skills and learned how to increase your mindfulness.

- You learned why it's important to identify emotions with emotional language and how it increases symptom management.

- You learned about the emotional and rational minds and walked the path to find the balance between the two, referred to as wise mind.

- You learned what skills you needed to step into wise mind and how you needed to use them to stay in your safe mental space.

- You learned the importance of creating physical, emotional, and mental space, as well as setting routines.

- You evaluated yourself, explored your mind, and assessed your skills and things you want to work on to think in a whole new way.

CHAPTER 3

DBT Module: Distress Tolerance

I have a solid foundation and am more confident. I am better prepared to take responsibility to manage my distress symptoms with skills and support.

In this chapter, you'll learn about distress tolerance and how it helps with crisis responses in difficult situations. You'll do a self-evaluation to compare coping strategies and then explore real-life examples of how to apply healthy coping strategies. We'll also look at distraction techniques and how to soothe the senses when the nervous system has a distress response. The exercises throughout will help you reinforce your knowledge and keep you thinking about what you're doing and how to shift toward consistent skill use. Next, we'll dive into how to replace harmful behaviors with additional strategies and skills. Then we'll explore how to work through other methods of coping with distressing situations with a seven-step skill set called IMPROVE. By the end of the chapter, you'll understand how to manage PTSD when distress is elevated by focusing on calm body skills to address self-care and to regulate physical responses.

What Is Distress Tolerance?

Distress tolerance, or the ability to mindfully hold elevated levels of upset, is the next step after mindfulness skills. It encourages you to accept upsetting experiences in a nonjudgmental way, be in an environment without attempting to change it, and hold the emotions without attempting to stop or control what you are experiencing.

There is always an acceptance level with the use of these skills, but distress tolerance focuses more on facing reality rather than approving of what is occurring in the reality. With PTSD, responses are often reactive and overly emotional, which creates distress that is unmanageable and difficult to withstand. Our lives aren't filled solely with joy but also with significant pain and distress resulting from challenges that aren't easily navigated and overcome without pain. But attempting to avoid the reality of these difficulties leads to suffering. Non-acceptance of pain is the mechanism for suffering and leads to increased upset, especially when you are experiencing trauma-level distress. Distress tolerance gives you the skills to regulate those painful thoughts and feelings. By using those skills continually, you'll find that those painful, human experiences will be easier to tolerate as you learn to accept life with all of its challenges.

DBT distress tolerance skills focus on calming the nervous system while learning to distract yourself in a healthy way. As you work through your feelings of distress or upset, use these strategies to improve moments within an experience. Once you've relieved the feelings of distress, you'll likely find it easier to choose to accept reality. This willingness is a complementary skill that allows the mind to shift perspective and remain open yet still be healthy and accept the unchangeable.

The Benefits of Crisis Survival Skills for PTSD

PTSD is challenging when a crisis is present. As we work to understand the difficulties of managing strong emotional responses, exploring the benefits of crisis survival skills may be helpful. The tendency to respond reactively comes from heightened stress levels during an event that has potentially harmful consequences. Crisis survival skills, such as those you're learning with DBT, allow for more control and the ability to regulate reactivity. As you begin to understand your distress responses, notice the behaviors you exhibit, the thoughts you have, and what you feel in your experiences. The crisis survival skills we will examine in this chapter are in the second DBT module, distress tolerance, and they support withstanding severe responses including self-harm and suicidal urges while managing distress. Earlier in this workbook, we discussed the inability to identify skills to reduce that adrenaline alarm to the nervous system, which allows people with PTSD to react in times of distress.

With consistent use, survival skills for PTSD help reduce the sensory overload and may reduce reaction to stimuli. Crisis survival skills must be a part of a self-care plan to make them effective. Additional benefits may include less irritability, better coping through healthy distractions, and the ability to accept the things that are extremely challenging to resolve.

Evaluating Unhealthy Coping Strategies

Below is a list of unhealthy ways to cope with crises and distress. Check the coping skills you have used when distressed.

☐ I take extra medication or drink when I sense stress or a crisis.

☐ I go into "panic mode" when things feel like a crisis.

☐ I avoid conflict.

☐ I feel compelled to get closure in relationships.

☐ I can't accept change.

☐ My emotions overwhelm me, and I begin shaking in crisis situations.

☐ I don't like to be comforted by anyone when I am upset or distressed.

☐ I have lost more than 10 hours of sleep in a week during a crisis.

☐ I can't eat when I am distressed.

☐ My thoughts don't stop, so I keep busy day and night and avoid sleep.

All the items on this list are unhealthy and ineffective. While they may have helped before you began reading this workbook, they are short-term solutions to a bigger problem.

Let's see how to find more effective (mindful) ways to cope with distress.

Crisis Survival Skills for Difficult Moments

We initially discussed the challenge of experiencing crises with PTSD and will now look at less intense events that remain difficult. Understanding that all events are not moments of crisis but rather moments of difficulty may help you see the benefit of working on skills when situations are less intense. This is how we will examine using crisis survival skills during difficult moments. To help you understand what difficult moments look like in real life, here are a few examples:

- While driving on the highway, another driver cuts you off in traffic. When you honk your horn to warn them, they make an obscene gesture and speed away.

- As you prepare to plan a much-needed vacation, you discover your request for time off has been denied, and two other employees have had their requests approved.

Although the above examples may seem distressing, each is considered a difficult moment. The importance of managing difficult moments is that symptoms—even a potential suicidal thought while in emotional mind—can quickly be deescalated and resolved *before* distress occurs. Let's clarify ways crisis survival skills can help in each example:

- In the first example, you can remind yourself that there are some people who drive aggressively and behave in hurtful ways. You don't have to absorb that hurt and can turn up the volume on your radio as a healthy distraction.

- In the second example, accept that the decision has been made and that you have emotions about the choice that was made. You can imagine yourself eventually going on the vacation and instead plan a staycation or weekend visits to places you enjoy. You can reflect on how you may save money doing this.

Hopefully, this creates a clear image of difficult moments compared to distress. These crisis survival skills are explained in the next section.

Distraction

As we discussed earlier, the more significant issues with trauma are the strong responses you experience from prior traumatic events. These post-traumatic stress responses require skill use, including distraction. In this section, you'll learn healthy distraction methods and how to create a routine to prevent and reduce PTSD symptoms. Healthy distractions are the opposite of self-destructive behaviors. Earlier we discussed how PTSD relates to self-injurious and addictive behaviors and strong suicidal tendencies. In this chapter, you'll learn how to better manage difficult moments in your life and experiences that feel like you are in a crisis. Using DBT skills that refocus your mind on managing your senses and learning how to gain perspective will shift your attention to solutions as you work on self-regulation during moments of distress. With consistent skill use, you will increase your distress tolerance as you allow yourself to distract from experiences you cannot change. Healthy distraction focuses on finding pleasure in activities that keep you growing and thriving while managing PTSD symptoms.

DISTRACTING YOURSELF WITH ACCEPTS

The acronym ACCEPTS is a healthy way to distract when you're in distress. The skills in this acronym are activities, contributing, comparisons, emotions, pushing away, thoughts, and sensations. Activities include participating in hobbies, calling a loved one, exercise, or other physical tasks like gardening, working or labor, and things that allow you to move. Contributing may be helping people, doing a random act of kindness, and volunteering for something you care about in your life. Comparisons allow you to identify with those who have similar or less fortunate circumstances to help increase gratitude for where you are. Emotions let you explore feelings that are different than you have experienced—watching a sad movie instead of a violent movie is an example. Pushing away or blocking the mind gives you the option of mentally distancing yourself from something that is painful in the moment. The painful issue may be revisited at a later time. Thoughts offer a healthy way to refocus with counting, reading, looking, or focusing on something that is pleasing or neutral in your mind. Sensations focus on sensory distraction with items like ice, warm showers, aromatherapy, or the volume and content of music.

Self-Destructive Strategies or Distraction Skills

Below is a list of healthy distractions, followed on the next page by self-destructive strategies and their potential consequences. In the box below each self-destructive strategy, write a healthier way to distract yourself taken from the list of healthier distraction skills. Indicate how you will apply this to your life.

HEALTHIER DISTRACTIONS

Exercising outdoors	Calling a friend	Speaking an affirmation	Journaling	Walking outside
Eating a healthy snack	Meditating	Taking an exercise class	Making a meal for your family	Finding places to volunteer online
Emailing a friend	Starting a blog	Looking at an Etsy shop online	Crafting	Dancing to your favorite song
Watching a funny cartoon	Making a shopping list	Writing a card or note to mail	Mailing the card or note	Writing your name in colored markers
Doodling	Playing a card game	Listening to music	Visiting a friend	Walking your pet

continued

continued from page 47

Self-Destructive Strategy	Potential Consequence
1. Thinking about a mistake you made a year ago.	Hurting yourself emotionally and staying mentally stuck.
Healthier Distraction:	**How Will I Apply This to My Life?**
2. Drinking or smoking when stressed.	Avoiding in the short-term knowing the distress will return in due time.
Healthier Distraction:	**How Will I Apply This to My Life?**
3. Not taking prescription medication as prescribed.	The doctor cannot manage your medication and it becomes ineffective.
Healthier Distraction:	**How Will I Apply This to My Life?**
4. Speaking judgmentally about yourself.	You get accustomed to being treated poorly and fear that others will begin to treat you poorly.
Healthier Distraction:	**How Will I Apply This to My Life?**
5. Refusing to forgive.	You put a barrier between yourself and others and, again, stay stuck.
Healthier Distraction:	**How Will I Apply This to My Life?**

I've Got a Plan

In this exercise, think of ways you can distract in a healthy way. The previous exercise limited you to specific choices, so now you get full control to get your plan started. You can use the examples from page 47 or create your own now that you have the idea. Start with 10 and when you're done, begin using them right away. You've got this, so work your plan!

1. ....

....

....

2. ....

....

....

3. ....

....

....

4. ....

....

....

5. ....

....

....

continued

continued from page 49

6. ....
   ....
   ....

7. ....
   ....
   ....

8. ....
   ....
   ....

9. ....
   ....
   ....

10. ....
    ....
    ....

Self-Soothing

Self-soothing is the ability to relax through distraction and calm yourself in a moment of distress. It focuses on the five senses: sight, hearing, touch, smell, and taste. The ability to relax and self-soothe is important for people with PTSD. Because the body activates more distress responses to stimuli, it makes regulation and stabilization difficult—being able to soothe yourself will greatly reduce those occurrences. Remember that distress releases excessive adrenaline to the body to prepare to fight or to run. Self-soothing and calming the body helps reduce this occurrence and allows for a different cycle to occur. Creating a self-soothe plan in a daily routine greatly benefits people with elevated levels of distress and panic responses. It's important to understand that this may be more difficult for some and easier for others, so always focus on what is effective for you. You may choose to work with a mental health or medical professional to ensure that your self-soothing plan is appropriate for your needs and effective and safe for you and your body.

DISTRACTING YOURSELF WITH THE FIVE SENSES

When experiencing distress, focus on soothing your sight, hearing, smell, taste, and touch. What you look at and how you experience what you see contributes to your level of calm. Seeing the colors of fall trees or taking a mindful walk in a park or neighborhood you enjoy offers perspective and teaches your system to take in beautiful things. Meditation music or nature sounds are things you can experience to enjoy self-soothing by hearing. You may also speak with someone who has a calming tone and brings you comfort.

Aromatherapy with varied scents and cooking or baking things you enjoy smelling may create or remind you of a positive memory. Taste extends the smell skill after you cook. Perhaps you enjoy chocolate or a cookie during the holidays. Making the experience of taste special is the key aspect of this skill. Baths, cuddling your favorite blanket or pet, wearing comfortable slippers, or grazing your fingers against your clothing before wearing it lets you connect with what you're touching and what is touching you to determine what soothes you.

Making Sense of Senses

One way to better understand how your senses function is to use observation and description skills (wise mind) to examine them. In the following table, choose one of the senses and mindfully focus your attention on that sense. Write a description of your experience in the box next to the sense. Then reflect on one thing you noticed about your response to this exercise in the last box.

	Observation and Description (Focus on what you experienced, where you were, etc.)	I noticed this about my response as a result of this exercise
Sight		
Smell		
Taste		
Sound		
Touch		

Reflecting on My Senses

Use the lines below to reflect on any symptoms, distress, or sensations that were pleasing to you to find what may offer you relief or what you choose to avoid.

Crisis Survival Skills for Curbing Harmful Behavior

We first spoke of crisis survival skills in the context of difficult moments using distraction and self-soothing. This section will explore how to survive the urge to harm through action. Below are a few real-life examples you may have experienced:

- While away at college, you find that your self-harm urges are increasing before each exam. You are unable to get an appointment at the campus counseling office and have been experiencing flashbacks and feel trapped until spring break.

- You notice that, during the winter months, you become more depressed, easily irritated, and have memories of family members that you have lost. You express that you "don't want to be here anymore."

These examples are more distressing than the examples we encountered in the previous section, and new skills are needed beyond difficult moments. With harm-related symptoms, we are far from wise mind and more inclined to be in emotional mind. We lose time to implement a skill before action and distress occurs. Let's clarify ways crisis survival skills can help in each example:

- In the first example, the harmful behavior is the urge to self-harm and is building quickly, which means no skills are being used to decrease the intensity. Using relaxation and focusing on one thing at a time may help the situation. Using a perspective skill, like STOP, which we will explore next, offers the time to find an additional skill. This is the benefit of using crisis survival skills before the urge is unmanageable and no support is available.

- The second example is challenging because the statement is vague, suggesting some type of implied harm. When in emotional mind, use a mindfulness skill and identify the facts. You may need support, so it's helpful to ask those who love you to offer what you need. Express your feelings fully to others using "I" language instead of "you" language. You may consider asking your loved one whether they currently have the capacity to support you to allow space for boundaries and help you feel more comfortable sharing fully with that person. Do what works, which may include honoring your loved ones during difficult moments during holidays or creating a new tradition that includes those you love.

Using STOP

STOP is a distress tolerance skill that focuses on allowing yourself time in order to gain perspective. This skill, like many of the skills you've learned, is an acronym, with each letter representing the four steps to use the skill: stop, take a step back, observe, and proceed mindfully. These skills were developed to increase your ability to briefly pause as you learn to avoid reacting. It's a helpful skill to allow you the safe space needed to process information. STOP supports other DBT skills, such as emotion regulation, while helping you stay in control and withstand distress. These skills will begin to integrate with one another, and you will see the similarities with mindfulness skills and this distress tolerance skill and why it's helpful for PTSD.

STOP

A healthy pause when you're distressed gives you time to rethink and regain control. When you stop in the moment when having a trauma response, you can work through situations differently. With consistent use, distress becomes manageable, and you can take the time you need to add the additional steps to the STOP skill.

TAKE A STEP BACK

Taking a step back gives you the time and space needed to use skills to calm the body and minimize impulsive decisions and behaviors. This skill encourages you to pause in the moment to regain control. By taking a step back, you have a moment to self-soothe to identify what you may need.

OBSERVE

Like observation in our WHAT skills, it's important to notice what is occurring within and outside of you. These are the detective skills we spoke of earlier in the workbook. Be sure to self-evaluate and focus on the who, what, when, and where to increase your ability to use the mindfulness skill and this distress tolerance skill collaboratively.

PROCEED MINDFULLY

The final step of the STOP skill is to proceed mindfully. This is similar to the mindfulness skill that we called participation. It prepares you for other skills, such as interpersonal effectiveness, as you will be better able to decide what to do and how you feel and to consider the thoughts and feelings of others, thereby decreasing isolation associated with PTSD.

STOP: Crisis Situation Investigation (CSI)

Describe a crisis situation that happened to you and what you did to handle or manage your distress. Then identify how you might have used the STOP skill to better manage the situation.

My crisis situation: ....

....

What symptoms did you have that indicated you were in distress?

....

....

What did you do to manage your distress symptoms?

....

....

What was the outcome? ....

Now imagine applying STOP in this scenario:

Stop: ....

....

Take a step back: ....

....

Observe: ....

....

Proceed mindfully: ....

....

STOP: Using What I Now Know

When a situation occurs this week that causes you to feel upset, use the same STOP strategy to work through it.

My crisis situation: _____

_____

What symptoms are you having that indicate distress? _____

_____

Now use STOP: 🛑

Stop: _____

_____

Take a step back: _____

_____

Observe: _____

_____

Proceed mindfully: _____

_____

Did you use any other DBT skills to manage your distress symptoms?

What was the outcome?

_____

_____

_____

IMPROVE-ing Your Situation

The acronym IMPROVE is another effective way to regulate distress. The skills in this acronym are: imagery, meaning, prayer, relaxation, one thing in the moment, vacation, and encouragement. As with the other distress tolerance skills, the goal is to manage moments of crisis in more effective ways while tolerating distress. Improving your situation isn't about changing the situation but rather increasing your ability to withstand the upset and distress you're experiencing.

The imagery skill involves using your mind and your imagination. Meaning is about identifying a possible benefit or purpose of painful experiences. With prayer, you might seek a connection and open your heart to something greater than yourself. For the relaxation skill, you can choose to train your muscles and your body to learn how to relax. One thing in the moment means keeping your complete attention on tasks. The vacation skill helps you mentally escape in a healthy way, similar to how you might behave when on vacation. And finally, the encouragement skill teaches you how to be your own cheerleader.

IMAGERY

Imagery creates an opportunity to relax and focus within the self. This skill focuses on visualizing yourself functioning in a better way and giving yourself permission to let your mind wander in a healthier way. Using imagery helps you deal with internal visual memories and painful emotions as you begin to see yourself having a better sense of control over a distressing emotion or a flash-back related to a traumatic event.

MEANING

Meaning is finding purpose in pain or identifying the value in traumatic experiences. For some with PTSD, this may be an aspect of reconciling values and reprioritizing issues in their lives. This does not mean that the trauma or harm you experienced was fated to happen or that you must find purpose in the event itself, but rather that accepting that the event happened allows you to move forward with your healing process and perhaps even find opportunities for growth. Meaning encompasses the ability to focus on positivism, the ability to find hope in experiences that feel hopeless. It creates a foundation to connect with others who have been able to identify their purpose in their pain and to support one another in a meaningful way.

PRAYER

Prayer is focusing on being open to something you consider greater than your-self, whether it be a religious deity or a powerful idea such as compassion or the forces of nature. The power of this skill is to identify something higher and more powerful than yourself. Prayer could mean anything from complex religious practices to simple affirmations, with the overall goal of surrendering to something that supports the weight of the pain you experience. This is especially important for someone with PTSD when they feel alone and isolated. The skill may reduce the tendency for self-harm and suicidality.

RELAXATION

Relaxation allows the body and the muscles to be retrained to develop the ability to release tension. Examples of relaxation include progressive relaxation exercises, which allow the body to control and release tension on command. Because of the behavioral responses to PTSD, relaxation helps the body learn that it's safe to let go of tension. This skill can offer a greater sense of control over distress and ways to manage pain related to trauma symptoms.

ONE THING IN THE MOMENT

One thing in the moment allows you to focus your complete attention on the here and now. This skill has also been referred to as *present moment awareness*, and it allows you to become more aware and intentional with what you're doing. Those who are frequently distracted due to PTSD symptoms may benefit as they learn to refocus on the here and now and not on the past when a traumatic event occurred.

VACATION

Vacation offers you an opportunity to take a brief mental break from tasks, obligations, everyday stressors, or elevating distress. Because it's brief, it differs from avoidance and is a healthy alternative to attempting to push through. A brief vacation may look like spending extra time resting, taking a mindful walk in the park, and indulging in something you enjoy for 30 to 60 minutes before resuming the task that may have triggered upset.

ENCOURAGEMENT

Encouragement is a challenging skill in some ways because it relates to focusing on yourself and not relying on others to make you feel good in moments of distress. The benefit of using this skill is learning to rely on yourself in moments where you may be alone or feel isolated. This type of encouragement is also referred to as positive self-talk and can be repeated as much as you need until your mind believes what you're saying.

I Can Be My Own Best Cheerleader

On the lines below, write five encouraging statements to be your own best cheerleader. Remember to focus on the moment (the here and now) and what you're doing better. Here's an example:

"At this moment, I am doing my best to take care of my mind by breathing deeply."

1. ....

....

....

2. ....

....

....

3. ....

....

....

4. ....

....

....

5. ....

....

....

Meaning in My Pain

Now that you have worked on encouraging yourself with the encouragement skill, let's focus on identifying meaning or purpose that has emerged from a traumatic experience in your life. Take a moment to focus on what you are first aware of, and don't force yourself to remember the details. Gently allow your mind to recall what it chooses and use that for this exercise. Once you've identified the experience, write a few sentences about it below:

....

....

....

....

....

Now identify whether you have learned, created, or valued anything from the experience. Focus on how it has helped or shaped the way you function in life or allowed you to connect with others in meaningful ways. With certain experiences, you may find it difficult or impossible to find purpose or meaning arising from the event, and that's okay—you can still focus on your current experience of moving forward toward growth and healing.

....

....

....

....

....

Additional Distress Tolerance Techniques for PTSD

The ability to accept reality and find the dialectic, or the balance, between wanting things to change and working toward acceptance is extremely difficult when you're in distress. The final two skills we'll explore in this chapter focus on that concept and will teach you to manage the intense heat in the body that arises from distress.

The first skill, radical acceptance, is often perceived as allowing someone to get away with a hurt, perhaps one that has caused trauma. But the intention of the skill is to allow for a choice, as with all the skills you're learning. The change is in the mindset, the perception, and the emotions related to what you're working toward accepting. This skill requires significant intention and energy and can be draining.

The second skill, TIPP, supports the difficulty with maintaining the emotional and psychological energy required when practicing radical acceptance. It's a soothing skill to quickly cool the body and regulate the heat to a more balanced level. These two skills can function independently or, like most DBT skills, in a collaborative way. You can't do skill work wrong unless you don't do it at all. The most important aspect of every skill is to find what you need and what works for you. When you're experiencing crisis or upset, or if you're working to make sense of something substantial, all the skills are important to use, so find what you remember, then radically accept that it's time to change.

Radical Acceptance

Radical acceptance is the ability to face your reality. The depth and breadth of acceptance can be more painful than everyday experiences that cause upset. This is the distress associated with radically accepting what is. The benefit of radically accepting what is, instead of fighting against the "it" that is happening, is that suffering will end. This is the gain of working through the pain—knowing that you now have the ability and strength to tolerate the distress and get to the mental and emotional place called acceptance.

The benefit of experiencing the emotions and thoughts associated with radical acceptance is the ability to offer compassion and empathy to yourself and those you love. What you may have thought about your emotions, especially with a traumatic past, will change in a way you may have never realized. An example is the grief associated with the death of a loved one. The empathy and compassion of those who survive such a loss is strengthened by their ability to radically accept the distress and trauma associated with the experience.

This allows for decreased suffering and the ability to connect with others who may need support and encouragement.

I Changed My Pain

On the lines below, use your DBT description skill, along with radical acceptance, to identify three painful situations that you were able to overcome. Focus on what you were willing and able to do (willingness) to radically accept the pain of your experience.

1. In this situation, I

2. In this situation, I

3. In this situation, I

I Can Buffer My Suffer or Get Stuck in the Muck

Now identify a recent situation that you feel unable to resolve and overcome. Use your wise mind skill to describe it in as much detail as possible so that it is visual in this moment. When you have the situation described, begin to use radical acceptance to shift your mind to change the way you perceive and look at this situation. Focus on a potential gain and the possibility of assigning a deeper meaning to what is happening.

1. In my current situation, ...

   ....

   ....

   ....

   ....

   ....

2. I can use radical acceptance in this way (identify one or two things you want to achieve using this DBT skill):

   ....

   ....

   ....

   - I can shift my mind in this way: ....

     ....

     ....

     ....

     ....

     ....

continued

continued from page 65

- I can change the way I perceive my current situation in this way:

  _____

  _____

  _____

  _____

  _____

  _____

- The gain as I see it could be: _____

  _____

  _____

  _____

  _____

  _____

- The deeper meaning of what is happening could be:

  _____

  _____

  _____

  _____

  _____

Using TIPP

With PTSD, sensory issues often occur with the nervous system. Using TIPP skills focuses on immediate relief to the nervous system to decrease distress signals and calm the body. The steps associated with TIPP are temperature, intense exercise, paced breathing, and paired muscle relaxation. These four steps work to cool the body's physical responses because distress is increasing the temperature in the body. As you become aware of what your body needs, knowing which step to take will be more beneficial. Choosing to use an ice pack on a day when you are experiencing chills due to distress is an example of a lack of self-awareness. It's integral to understand what you may or may not need when using TIPP. The objective of this skill is to calm the system, not to shock it. Let's look at how to use TIPP most effectively.

TEMPERATURE

To immediately calm the body, you can use the temperature skill to cool it. This skill supports decreasing elevated distress and may assist with dissociation and stabilizing mood. You can practice this skill with ice packs or cold compresses, by drinking and holding cold beverages, or by taking a cool shower.

INTENSE EXERCISE

When anxiety or panic is the cause of distress, the body needs to use that energy through intense exercise. It's important for PTSD symptoms to be managed in this way to avoid self-harm and harm to others when you are experiencing distress due to high reactivity.

PACED BREATHING

The goal of paced breathing is to regulate your nervous system, create calm, and increase your ability to focus and control your breath. By exhaling slower than you inhale, at a steady, rhythmic pace, you can reduce trauma symptoms because air is able to permeate the body using the full capacity of your lungs.

PAIRED MUSCLE RELAXATION

This skill is used with paced breathing to help your body understand how to manage tension. By tensing and relaxing, you are creating muscle memory. You're teaching the body that you're able to calm yourself and can instruct it to do so by simply using your breath and the natural rhythmic pulses occurring in the body.

Chill Out

In this exercise, you'll learn to calm the body using the temperature skill. For one week, use this skill at least once daily. Examples of ways to use this skill include having an ice-cold drink when distressed or taking a cool shower when you feel irritated or are experiencing elevated stress levels. Record your skill use below.

_____

_____

_____

_____

_____

_____

When you used this skill this week, how did it affect:

Your mood? _____

_____

Your thoughts? _____

_____

Your behaviors? _____

_____

Your relationships? _____

_____

Just for Today, Use Your Breath to Relax

In this exercise, choose one day to use the TIPP skill during the day to focus on your paced breathing with the paired muscle relaxation. You can use this skill at any time to help yourself relax.

Before using the exercise, plan how you will use your skills.

1. In which five locations do you think you want to use this skill? Do you plan to be alone, or will you need support?

....

....

....

....

....

2. Now practice using the paced breathing, focusing on inhaling for a count of five and exhaling for a count of seven. Repeat while moving to the next step.

3. Now practice using paired muscle relaxation by tensing your bicep, your fist, or your glutes. Hold for the count of five while you inhale and slowly release the muscle as you exhale.

4. Continue to breathe and control your muscles in this way for as long as you are comfortable.

5. When you choose to conclude the exercise, take a moment to reflect on how you feel in your mind and body.

....

....

....

....

....

Key Takeaways

Now you've learned the basics of distress tolerance and how it can be helpful when managing PTSD symptoms. Here are the key things you have learned from this chapter:

- You mastered several distress tolerance techniques and have practiced how each is used.

- You can identify the need for crisis survival skills when experiencing difficult moments or urges to act on harmful behaviors and when PTSD symptoms are activated.

- You completed a self-evaluation and identified better ways to deal with difficult experiences using distraction and self-soothing.

- You explored how to use the STOP and IMPROVE skills when distress occurs.

- You learned about radical acceptance and how it is helpful in managing distress.

- You explored the principles of the TIPP skill and how to use it to calm the body when feeling elevated stress levels.

CHAPTER 4

DBT Module: Emotion Regulation

I am now mindful and intentional in managing my distress. I confidently open myself to the gift of emotional control to understand the messages being conveyed to me.

This chapter will introduce you to emotion regulation skills. Using the WHAT skills from chapter 2, you will learn to identify and name emotions and what they mean. More specifically, you'll decipher how to understand your emotions and regulate them to find emotional balance. Building on the skills from the previous chapters, you will learn how to further manage PTSD symptoms and address the crisis responses when you experience strong reactive urges. We will identify the benefit of emotion regulation related to crises, and then you'll complete a self-evaluation of unhealthy emotional urges that prompt reactions. To help you understand healthy strategies, we will explore ways to focus on positivity, build mastery, decrease vulnerabilities, and cope better when you're emotionally dysregulated or distressed. As you progress, you'll apply each skill practically by completing exercises as you add them to your daily routine.

The chapter concludes with a meditation to reinforce how to be kind to yourself and how to increase perspective about relationships. By the end of this chapter, you will increase your skill use, and you'll be well prepared to dive into the final module in chapter 5. There you will see the connections between modules and skill used as you achieve mastery in your everyday routine.

What Is Emotion Regulation?

You may understand what an emotion is yet be unsure how to control it. Emotion regulation uses core mindfulness to increase your ability to observe, describe, and recognize the emotion experienced. Although you may have experienced many painful emotions—as is expected with PTSD symptoms—there are also positive emotions that you may not know. This is why it's important to not only explore the painful feelings but also discover new, more pleasant emotions. In chapter 2, we discussed the three states of mind, one of them being emotional mind. This chapter will help you regulate your emotions and walk the path to wise mind. This is done with the distress tolerance skills you learned in chapter 3, particularly radical acceptance, in which letting go reduces your suffering. Understanding that core mindfulness skills have helped you regain control of your state of mind, emotion regulation helps you challenge and reframe negative thoughts. As you increase positive experiences, you will have more positive emotions. Consistent emotion regulation means you will be less vulnerable to being in emotional mind and distress.

As discussed in chapter 2, using mindfulness and distress tolerance skills consistently and with a routine gives you the support to build on your skills. So again, work with the routine you created. You can always modify your routine in a way that works for you. Just keep using all your skills. In this chapter, you will learn how to love and feel healthy and balanced. You will learn the emotions that you may have felt when symptomatic, such as anger, sadness, and depression. You may have not understood why you felt many of these emotions while never feeling other emotions. This is the benefit of emotion regulation—what you are aware of, you are better able to control.

The Benefits of Emotion Regulation for PTSD

The intense response that occurs when distress is triggered or activated is called *emotional dysregulation*. This emotional state causes a sense of being out of control and a feeling of imbalance. It's also when you may be in emotional mind and unable to make sense of your experience, reducing your skill use. Balanced emotions are needed to regulate your distress and get to wise mind. You may recall a time when you faced distress that caused anger, depression, or panic and had no skill to make sense to yourself or others. As you continue to work through this chapter, you'll see that emotion regulation allows you to find emotional balance and stability to cope with the distressing situation that caused those emotions.

As you discovered in chapter 2, using mindfulness skills also supports better symptom management. In this chapter, you'll identify how mindfulness and emotion regulation skills help you not only understand the present moment but have the emotional stability to be more effective (yet another mindfulness skill).

Soon, you'll be able to identify experiences where you can apply emotion regulation benefits in your life as you work through more introspective exercises with each skill. It's time for another self-check to see where you may be struggling. Let's take a look at your level of dependence on unhealthy emotional urges in the following self-evaluation.

Evaluating Unhealthy Emotional Urges

Being able to identify what you consider unhealthy will allow you to target where to start working on regulating your emotions. In the table below, you will identify your targets by thinking about times that you have acted on your emotions in an unhealthy way. In the first column, write five emotions that you struggle with that cause emotional imbalance resulting in an unhealthy urge or behavior. In the second column, write the urge or behavior associated with the emotion on the left. This may be a behavior or urge that you want to manage or that you want to change. Review what you've written and consider using these five emotions for future exercises in this workbook.

Emotion	Unhealthy urge or behavior

Decreasing Emotional Vulnerabilities with ABC

We all struggle with our emotions from time to time and are vulnerable to moments of upset. Being able to work through these moments before distress occurs is important to decreasing our vulnerability to emotional upset. To prevent this unwanted type of emotional vulnerability, the key is to work toward minimizing occurrences of upsetting, distressing experiences. As we work through understanding the words that describe our feelings, we can reduce the tendency to function from emotional mind, making it easier to know how to proceed. The best way to do that is to use the ABC skills, which are: accumulate positives, build mastery, and coping ahead.

Read Roberta's story to gain a better understanding.

A VULNERABLE MOMENT

Roberta struggles with PTSD and admits to being frustrated and having anger issues. She attends therapy with a DBT-certified therapist but reports that therapy isn't working, and she wants to quit.

Roberta has strong emotions and is unable to effectively describe her feelings. She has the urge to quit due to her frustration, which is a typical response when we feel stuck. It seems Roberta doesn't understand that, but DBT therapists are trained to offer supportive skills to help people like Roberta identify what they need. Roberta's therapist encourages her to use the DBT ABCs and to refocus on using her skills to resist the urge to quit. Roberta discusses how she can better accumulate more positive experiences in her life, focus on building mastery with things she can control, and practice seeing herself coping differently. By the end of the session, Roberta is able to think about taking a vacation, doing gardening, and getting more sleep.

In the example, you may understand the emotions Roberta felt and perhaps have identified similar feelings of anger and frustration in the self-evaluation you did earlier. There are and will be occasions when you need support with identifying your needs and wants as opposed to your urges and reactions. As we move forward with emotion regulation, you will see how decreasing vulnerability to urges using your DBT ABCs will help you, as it helped our friend Roberta.

Accumulate Positives

The first skill in the DBT ABCs is to accumulate or find as many positives as possible. This means you're seeking your strengths or finding the "silver lining in the clouds." Please understand that just because you can't see the silver lining doesn't mean it doesn't exist. You simply have to seek it and work for it. This is the point of accumulating your positives.

The benefit of seeking positives is feeling joy and gratitude for all the things you may not have realized you have going for you in your everyday life. If you find that life seems cloudy and there is no silver lining, your challenge is to take the opportunity to *create* positive experiences on your own terms and within your control. When you identify reasons to live and to work toward a vision for your life each day, your emotions will offer you hope in exchange for trauma.

Finding My Silver Lining

Identify five things in your life that seem bleak or dreary. These are your clouds. To practice finding the silver lining, identify at least one thing that you've learned, gained, or are grateful for as a result of these clouds.

Build Mastery

Finding things that you do well may be a challenge. Trauma responses related to PTSD make it difficult to identify the small things you are confident about, especially when it seems you've been unsuccessful in the past. That doesn't mean it's not achievable—it may just mean that your symptoms, especially the emotional responses, tell you that you can't.

The build mastery skill is how you can challenge your emotional mind when your symptoms are increasing. Building mastery means focusing on things that allow you to feel confident, in control, and capable. Exchange things that are too difficult or too challenging for something that you do well. Maybe you're an amazing artist, and when you sketch or paint, you have feelings that allow you freedom and control to create. Most of us have some form of creativity that is a solid first step to using this skill. Challenge yourself to find that creative thing that increases your confidence, allows you to feel in control, and gives you the emotional balance to feel capable.

This skill will be easy to remember since there are five Cs in it:

- Confident

- Control

- Capable

- Creative

- Challenge yourself

The Five Cs of Building Mastery

Think about the five Cs of building mastery: confident, control, capable, creative, and challenging yourself. In this exercise, you'll identify one way you are doing each of the steps in this skill. Be descriptive and challenge what you think you know about yourself.

Steps to Building Mastery	How I Am Building Mastery in My Life
Confident	
Control	
Capable	
Creative	
Challenge Yourself	

Coping Ahead

This skill focuses you on the present moment and what you're able to do now. As you increase your emotional balance, it becomes easier to visualize yourself being more in control of your life. Coping ahead gives you time in the present to see the person you want to be. With this skill, you can begin rehearsing how to do that in a more effective way. You may also use rehearsal—such as role playing how and when to use your skills—to prevent traumatic experiences that may challenge the control you have with your emotions.

With support and encouragement, it becomes easier to find the problem and work through the insecurities and doubt when situations are emotional. Using coping ahead makes it easier for you to regulate emotions by practicing before a situation occurs. The result is reduced vulnerability to emotional upset as you become better able to maintain self-control with the skills needed for each situation.

Playing the Role

Pietro has a history of childhood abuse, and now as an adult, he isolates and admits to having low self-esteem. Pietro frequently tries a variety of jobs and has just told his DBT-certified therapist, "I'm a fantastic failure. I don't know why I even bother to try."

Pietro's trauma is prompting emotional, negative self-talk, and he's using a "mindless" phrase, *try*. Once Pietro understands what he has been feeling, he states that he is often overwhelmed and makes mistakes, resulting in write-ups and threats of termination from each job. His therapist can now identify Pietro's issue, which is that he has not been able to find his confidence in the workplace and is often functioning mindlessly. Now that Pietro understands his problem, he and his therapist can role play situations by coping ahead to prevent the emotional threat of termination from a job. By the end of the session, Pietro focuses on being more mindful and using positive self-talk when feeling insecure doing work tasks.

Name three additional emotion regulation skills Pietro may use and identify how they can help:

1. ....

    ....

    ....

2. ....

    ....

    ....

3. ....

    ....

    ....

    ....

Your Role Play

Now that you understand how to connect building mastery and coping ahead, think of a time when you struggled, like Pietro did in the previous exercise. Write your narrative, identifying where you may be stuck and how you might use role play or rehearsal to solve your problem. Remember to use wise mind, and if you need support to work through the exercise, this is a way to prepare for your therapy session or to talk it over with a trusted friend.

Decreasing Emotional Vulnerabilities with PLEASE

The acronym PLEASE is a healthy way to reduce emotional vulnerabilities through self-awareness, self-validation, and self-care. This skill set is especially important for those who have difficulty identifying emotions and expressing their needs due to PTSD symptoms. Often the fear of not having needs met due to neglect or being disappointed may be why we fail to attend to our needs. PLEASE skills focus on the imbalances and vulnerabilities that must be considered to reduce emotional dysregulation. Each step will teach you to elevate your awareness and experience the benefits of attending to your self-care. The steps in the acronym PLEASE are **P**hysical i**L**lness, (balanced) **E**ating, **A**voiding mood-altering substances, (balanced) **S**leep, and **E**xercise.

Treating physical illness focuses on being aware of vulnerabilities related to your body, mind, and emotions and a lack of resources both past and present. Balanced eating includes identifying foods that support your wellness and are balanced and portioned to support what your body needs to function safely. By avoiding mood-altering substances, such as alcohol or unprescribed medications, you decrease the vulnerability to emotional dysregulation. Well-balanced sleep helps you learn to relax and calms the body while clearing your emotions during rest. A healthy exercise routine gives you movement to stimulate the mind and elevates mood. Building mastery is a skill that helps you feel success and increases self-esteem and self-worth. Being in control and feeling capable and confident also offer mental health benefits.

PL: Physical Illness

Attending to physical illness includes being aware of any and all vulnerabilities related to your body (physical), your mind and mental state (psychological), your feelings (emotional), not having what you need to survive (a lack of supports or resources), or other aspects of illnesses in your life from your past or in the present. The key to understanding this skill is asking yourself, "What do I need that I lack or haven't had to be my best self?" We often think of illness as being sick, and while that is a part of this skill, we must consider all the categories that cause us to feel sick, weak, or unlike our best self.

The BE PLEASED Pyramid

You have just learned the part of the PLEASE skill that focuses on physical illness, and the acronym contains other categories related to your overall health and the vulnerabilities you may not have realized. Below is a pyramid that contains each letter in the PLEASE skill (along with B, E, and D, to form BE PLEASED) to help you see that everything must be balanced to support your well-being as you continue to reduce your emotional vulnerabilities. Use each letter to think of ways you can BE PLEASED in one or two short sentences. Since B, E, and D aren't in the original PLEASE acronym, feel free to think up emotional regulation strategies (corresponding to those letters or not) that apply to you.

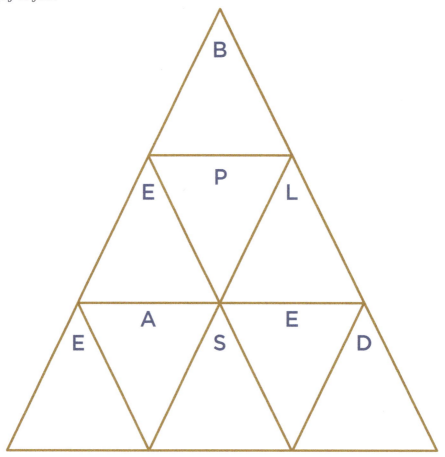

E: (Balanced) Eating

We know that the food we eat not only tastes good but also fuels the body to keep all its parts functioning. Sometimes we forget that when we overeat, forget to eat, or undereat, we do the body harm. As a result, our emotions become unbalanced because our intake is imbalanced.

The key to using this skill is to mindfully eat by understanding what food makes you feel stable, strong, and healthy. You may have to ask yourself, "How do I feel when I drink this beverage and when I eat this type of food?" This skill relies on your mindfulness skills (WHAT and HOW, specifically) to make wise food choices. Remember that your body is a wonderful gift that helps you work on managing your thoughts, emotions, physical health, and all the special things that make you who you are.

Taste Something New

In this exercise, you'll taste 20 foods. Sounds exciting, right? It can be, depending on how you look at it, and I hope you see this as a way to find out how you respond to taste and the effect it has on mood. Mood and food are related and affect each other. When we discussed how to be stable, healthy, and strong, you were asked to reflect on how you feel when eating certain foods. This is where you get to put that idea to the test. In the table below is a list of 20 foods you can test. Pick from the list or use the lines below the choices in the table to write in your own foods. Then write how you feel after you eat what you've chosen. You may find you enjoy a new food or that you really don't. Be brave and see what happens with your emotions. Most of all, have fun and eat!

MY FOOD MOOD CHART							
Food	Mood	Food	Mood	Food	Mood	Food	Mood
Apple		Brown rice		Fish		Nuts	
Avocado		Cabbage		Garlic		Onions	
Banana		Carrots		Ginger		Pear	
Beans		Celery		Kale		Peppers	
Broccoli		Chicken		Lemon		Sweet potato	

A: Avoiding Mood-Altering Substances

Although we discussed avoidance as a harmful behavior, avoidance is necessary when considering the use of alcohol and drugs, which alter the mood and emotions. It's understandable that, when you're struggling with overwhelming panic and fear associated with PTSD symptoms, there is a need for immediate relief from distress and overwhelming emotions. But using non-prescription mood-altering drugs is harmful when you're attempting to balance the emotions.

This skill requires you to accept the challenge of avoiding drugs that alter your mood in exchange for working through the emotions that require your attention. Remember that your emotions are communicators, and if you use mood-altering drugs, you will miss the message.

Mood-Altering or Mood Momentum

In this exercise, you can see how mood-altering substances can cause distress. You now know that our thoughts and emotions influence our desire to act. Think of a time when you went through this cycle. Then reflect on how you've now learned how to overcome a challenging experience and used mood momentum—performing balanced behaviors to create and maintain positive moods. It may take a while to recall a memory; however, it may be simple, such as petting your cat or dog instead of having a drink. The simple experiences can bring the most fulfillment and joy.

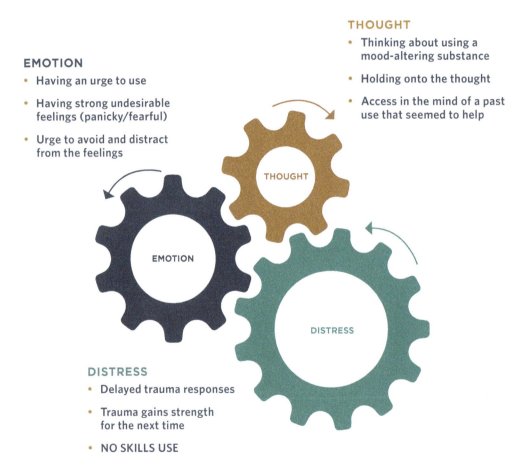

THOUGHT
- Thinking about using a mood-altering substance
- Holding onto the thought
- Access in the mind of a past use that seemed to help

EMOTION
- Having an urge to use
- Having strong undesirable feelings (panicky/fearful)
- Urge to avoid and distract from the feelings

DISTRESS
- Delayed trauma responses
- Trauma gains strength for the next time
- NO SKILLS USE

S: (Balanced) Sleep

Your body benefits from balanced eating, and it needs to rest in order to use those balanced meals you ate. As food fuels the body, sleep heals your system, removing and placing memories where they belong, allowing you to dream, and, eventually, relax.

While you may be concerned about PTSD symptoms challenging your sleep and rest due to nightmares and flashbacks, when you plan your sleep, your body will learn when it's time to relax. You can use the skills we've explored to help work through your distress. The benefit of a sleep hygiene routine helps you train your body to relax and be calm as it prepares for the rest it deserves after a hard day's work.

Sleep Hygiene Routine

Sleep hygiene is the preparation and planning before attempting sleep. It is an attempt to create structure and a routine to prepare the brain and body to relax. This is especially challenging for people with PTSD since calming the body is difficult. In this exercise, you will create a sleep hygiene routine.

Using visualization and imagery (your IMPROVE skill), picture yourself planning for the event called sleep. Treat yourself like a baby, since that is often the last time many of us have had a sleep routine. Write 10 steps on the lines below and complete them for one week. Check off each step as you complete it.

	Sun	Mon	Tues	Wed	Thur	Fri	Sat
1.							
2.							
3.							
4.							
5.							
6.							
7.							
8.							
9.							
10.							

E: Exercise

You've already learned how you're more likely to benefit from skills if you practice them consistently. What you may not know yet is that creating and sticking with an exercise routine frequently results in a happy feeling in your brain. The chemical that creates this emotion is called serotonin, which feels amazing. And you can activate it without a prescription. The only thing you need to do is move.

When you start an exercise routine, it may feel emotional, but the chart in the following exercise will help you identify how you're progressing. Remember that it takes about four weeks to make significant changes. With consistency, exercise will become part of your healthy routine.

My Own Antidepressant

Now that you understand the benefits of exercising your body, you will exercise your mind. Identify how you feel before and after you exercise by using the following chart, and be sure to start on the same day each week. I'm sure you'll see that your mood is elevated, your sleep more restful, and your trauma responses lessened.

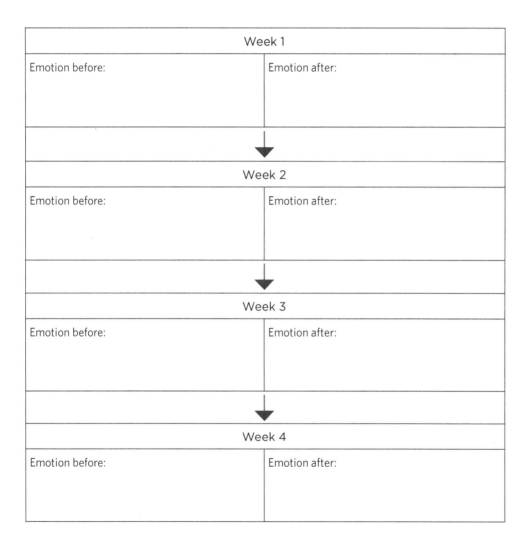

Week 1	
Emotion before:	Emotion after:

Week 2	
Emotion before:	Emotion after:

Week 3	
Emotion before:	Emotion after:

Week 4	
Emotion before:	Emotion after:

Additional Emotion Regulation Techniques for PTSD

We're now going to explore additional emotion regulation skills and the techniques to apply them to PTSD. The first skill is opposite action, also called *opposite to emotion*. This skill encourages you to better understand your mood as it relates to your behaviors. You may have struggles with self-care, including a lack of sleep, imbalanced eating, and other emotional vulnerabilities. The result is poor decision-making due to an inability to work through the emotions and thoughts that keep us stuck. The more we avoid using emotion regulation strategies, the more suffering occurs. You'll learn to face the emotion to find its opposite. This will help you get unstuck and make highly effective choices.

The next skill is being kind to yourself. Seems simple, yet it may be one of the most challenging skills you'll learn to put into practice. A common theme with those diagnosed with PTSD is difficulty being gentle, kind, and forgiving. This doesn't apply to others as much as it does to forgiving yourself. But by working on yourself, you are in the process of undoing that behavior, so please be proud of that.

Another skill you'll learn is to reappraise your emotions. This will shift the way you think about aspects of your life and help with general well-being and interpersonal relationships. The final skill is adopting healthy self-soothing rituals. We explored self-soothing when distressed, and we are now creating a routine to calm the body when emotions present themselves.

Practicing Opposite to Emotion and Opposite Action

People with PTSD symptoms may be unable to understand challenging or difficult emotions. The skill of identifying opposite action or opposite to emotion helps you acknowledge the emotion that is presenting in order to find its opposite. Many of the issues we discussed—such as imbalances with sleeping, eating, or not exercising—increase the difficulty with identifying the emotion and finding its opposite. When dealing with fear responses, it is important to identify the fear without avoidance in order to work through the distress. Practicing opposite action allows you to do that with all emotions that may be stressful or distressing.

Opposite to Emotion

In this exercise, you're going to test what you have learned about emotions. In chapter 2, you completed the Minding My Emotional Mind exercise (see page 18) and identified the names of your feelings. Now that you have command of the words, let's find the opposite emotion. If you prefer, you can write more than one emotion on the line to find your way to the opposite. Do your best and check the answers in the back of this workbook when you're finished (see page 164).

EXAMPLE: STRESSED ⟶ CALM

1. Depressed ⟶ ....

2. Afraid ⟶ ....

3. Bored ⟶ ....

4. Confident ⟶ ....

5. Worried ⟶ ....

6. Scared ⟶ ....

7. Shy ⟶ ....

8. Exhausted ⟶ ....

9. Hysterical ⟶ ....

10. Jealous ⟶ ....

Being Kind to Yourself

When we discussed mindfulness in earlier chapters, loving kindness was mentioned as a way to show compassion to yourself and others. Loving kindness is just what it says: the ability to offer love and kindness. As an addition to the emotion regulation skills you've already learned in this chapter, we will now focus on extending this kindness to yourself.

Whether you offer yourself a compliment, say your affirmations daily, or use self-soothing skills, you'll be offering kindness to yourself with each exercise you are completing. Many struggles with PTSD come from increased self-judgment and less compassion and forgiveness for yourself when working through the challenges that symptoms present. As you allow yourself time to learn and grow from your traumatic experiences, you are starting the process of being kind and patient with yourself.

The Art of Loving Kindness

Follow this guided meditation to practice the art of loving kindness toward yourself. As with all meditations, remember to focus on smooth, continuous breathing (see TIPP, page 67). Speak with intention and focus, opening your heart to offer love and kindness to yourself.

1. Find a comfortable, relaxed posture in a safe space.

2. Using paced breathing, focus on inhaling for a count of five and exhaling for a count of seven. Continue breathing in this way as you move to the next steps.

3. Focus your intention on sending loving kindness to those you find difficult to love.

4. Repeat slowly to yourself or out loud: *May you be at peace. May your heart be open. May you be aware of the light of your own true nature. May you be healed. May you be a source of healing for all souls.*

5. Now repeat to those who you may have caused pain, without guilt or shame: *May you be at peace. May your heart be open. May you be aware of the light of your own true nature. May you be healed. May you be a source of healing for all souls.*

6. Let go of your self-judgment and everything that has blocked your heart. Focus on allowing yourself to be forgiven.

7. Now direct loving kindness to yourself as you continue to follow your breath and focus your intention on compassion.

8. Repeat the following: *May I be at peace. May I be open. May I be open to the light of my own true nature. May I be healed. May I be a source of healing for all souls.*

9. Breathe comfortably as you receive kindness and gently sit with a new feeling of compassion.

10. When you're ready, gently open your eyes.

This meditation is taken from "The Art of Loving Kindness" from *Blissfully by Dr. V* on SoundCloud.

Reappraising Your Feelings

As a jeweler appraises the value of a diamond and initially has an emotional reaction based on what is observed, so do we also find the value in our feelings through appraisal.

The first thoughts we have, and the emotional responses associated with those thoughts, are what happen when we have experienced a traumatic event. The ability to look at a situation and reappraise it with facts, using mindfulness skills, challenges the way you view and think about your thoughts, experiences, emotions, and trauma.

This is how to gain perspective as you work through challenging emotions and thoughts. Initially, you may get stuck with your thoughts and your feelings, but, with time, you'll learn to use reappraisal for a powerful outlook on your life.

Help Reappraise Rosa's Anger

In this exercise, you will help Rosa to use the reappraisal skills you have just mastered. Rosa's cycle of anger is listed below, and she is stuck. Give Rosa reappraisals at each stage of her cycle of anger to give her a fresh perspective.

ROSA'S CYCLE OF ANGER:

Event ("My friend was late for brunch and told me it was due to slow traffic.")

Thoughts ("My friend was late because I'm not important." "This always happens to me.")

Emotions (irritation, annoyance, anger, rage)

Body symptoms (shaking, neck tension, heaving breathing, heart palpitating)

Behavior (arguing, yelling, not talking, not eating)

How can you help Rosa reappraise so that she can see things with facts?

_____

_____

_____

_____

_____

Adopting Healthy Self-Soothing Rituals

In chapter 3, we discussed using self-soothing to relax through healthy distraction in times of distress. You have learned that with PTSD the body activates more distress, making emotion regulation difficult.

Self-soothing is the skill that helps us learn how we can calm the body. Self-soothing rituals will focus on your five senses and are done with intention. This means you make it a part of your routine, have what you need, and plan it clearly. Self-soothing the body in this way signals it to expect to calm, so it will create a new cycle of calm. By using a self-soothe ritual in your daily routine, you'll reduce your elevated levels of emotional distress and panic and achieve calm.

Creating a Self-Soothe Ritual

Now that you have the skill to self-soothe and the ability to use a routine, let's work on a ritual to bring all three skills together. You have awareness of what you need and want, so it will be easy for you to identify what you need for the self-soothe ritual. Respond to the questions and statements below to get you thinking about what you need and how to plan for your self-soothe ritual.

1. What do you want to do to self-soothe?

2. What three things do you need to self-soothe?

3. How often do you want to do your self-soothe ritual?

4. What do you lack that might keep you from committing to your self-soothe ritual?

5. What do you have going for you that will keep you using this self-soothe ritual?

6. When do you plan to begin?

Now that you've completed the questions, schedule time to get what you need and to begin your self-soothe ritual.

Key Takeaways

Great job! You've completed the fourth chapter, and you're approaching the final module of DBT. In this chapter, you worked on emotion regulation and learned how to manage intense emotional responses. Let's focus on the specifics you can take away from it:

- You learned what emotion regulation is and how it benefits managing the emotions related to PTSD.

- You did another self-evaluation to identify unhealthy urges as you prepared to work through some of those behaviors and responses.

- You learned your DBT ABCs to decrease your vulnerability to emotional distress.

- You learned how to BE PLEASED and focused on the importance of attending to vulnerabilities like physical illness and to identify other types of illness using DBT.

- You discovered ways to balance eating, sleep, and exercise, while avoiding mood-altering substances.

- You explored four additional skills, including opposite emotion and action, offering kindness to yourself, giving time to reappraise your feelings, and creating a ritual to self-soothe.

- You learned what skills you needed to step into a calm, emotional space and to maintain it.

CHAPTER 5

DBT Module: Interpersonal Effectiveness

I acknowledge that I need others and am not alone in this world. As I move forward, I will choose to engage in healthy and respectful relationships.

This chapter focuses on your final DBT module, interpersonal effectiveness, which will teach you ways to relate to others as you attend to your own needs. With interpersonal effectiveness skills, you'll understand how the DBT modules work together. You will also learn how to have supportive and healthy relationships that focus on mutual respect. We'll identify the benefit of using interpersonal effectiveness skills in everyday situations and crises, and you'll complete a self-evaluation to find your communication style. This chapter will also explore healthy methods of communicating your wants and needs using assertive communication when offering and receiving respect and learning how to disagree safely. Building on your knowledge from earlier chapters, this one will equip you with the remaining skills you need to help reduce your PTSD symptoms using DBT. You'll also find several exercises throughout to give you more practice to support your skill use. As you conclude chapter 5, you'll start to integrate your mindfulness, distress tolerance, emotional regulation, and interpersonal effectiveness skills. Let's get started!

What Is Interpersonal Effectiveness?

Interpersonal effectiveness skills empower you to establish and sustain existing friendships and relationships, while you explore methods of working through difficulties that challenge those relationships. By using these skills, you'll be better equipped to ask for what you need and offer and receive respect. Interpersonal effectiveness skills also help you be more aware of how and when to set boundaries and how to do so in a way that is emotionally balanced and mindful. As you learn to function in balanced relationships, you are better able to create healthier ways of responding to others and ensure you feel safe and understood. This may be a new concept to you, especially if you've struggled with feeling alone as a result of trauma and distress. Remember that it just takes practice.

One key aspect of interpersonal effectiveness is that you'll learn to be more assertive and comfortable with saying no to requests when it feels unsafe for you. As we've learned with emotion regulation skills, it's important to understand how being assertive in relationships may be emotional and challenging for you. Please know that this is a normal response, and it takes time to make changes and work through these challenges. You may have been reactive and judgmental in the past or felt judged in prior relationships. If we take a moment to understand that you may have felt unsafe as a result of your experiences and did not have the skills to work through those unsafe relationships, you may have a different viewpoint. As you work through this chapter, use the skills from the prior chapter to help you identify how you have struggled with those you encountered and ways to make relationships less painful as you grow more skillful. This is the benefit of interpersonal effectiveness.

The Benefits of Interpersonal Effectiveness for PTSD

There are many benefits of learning and using the skills within the interpersonal effectiveness module. Because you are aware of what PTSD is, you can easily identify the barriers when you're experiencing strong emotional responses while communicating in relationships. These challenges occur when you're experiencing distress and emotional dysregulation, frequently resulting in misunderstandings and strained relationships. A trauma response could be giving an ultimatum in the relationship to your loved one to avoid the fear of rejection. Using interpersonal effectiveness skills increases your ability to "hold" an emotion until those responses can be resolved with a distress tolerance skill.

Another benefit of interpersonal effectiveness includes learning your communication style. There are four main types of communication styles that we all use in interpersonal interactions: passive, aggressive, passive-aggressive, or assertive. It's important to note that no one style is good or bad, which is why we use a dialectical approach to understand how and when to use these communication styles. Each of us has one that we gravitate more toward and that may be a default due to trauma, culture, or how we were raised. In the following exercise, you will increase your understanding of your own communication style.

Understanding Your Communication Style

Below is a list of common statements that you may have used or have heard others use when communicating with you. Circle which communication style is being used. When you have finished, see if you can identify your own communication style based on the statements you examined. The answer key is in the back of the workbook (see page 165).

1.	I feel tired and need a cup of tea.	PASSIVE	AGGRESSIVE	ASSERTIVE	PASSIVE-AGGRESSIVE
2.	I wish I had someone to take care of me.	PASSIVE	AGGRESSIVE	ASSERTIVE	PASSIVE-AGGRESSIVE
3.	Nobody ever asks me how I'm doing.	PASSIVE	AGGRESSIVE	ASSERTIVE	PASSIVE-AGGRESSIVE
4.	Everybody is out to get me.	PASSIVE	AGGRESSIVE	ASSERTIVE	PASSIVE-AGGRESSIVE
5.	I can't believe no one cleaned this kitchen!	PASSIVE	AGGRESSIVE	ASSERTIVE	PASSIVE-AGGRESSIVE
6.	I'm glad somebody understands me.	PASSIVE	AGGRESSIVE	ASSERTIVE	PASSIVE-AGGRESSIVE
7.	Whatever.	PASSIVE	AGGRESSIVE	ASSERTIVE	PASSIVE-AGGRESSIVE
8.	Who cares?	PASSIVE	AGGRESSIVE	ASSERTIVE	PASSIVE-AGGRESSIVE
9.	It is what it is.	PASSIVE	AGGRESSIVE	ASSERTIVE	PASSIVE-AGGRESSIVE
10.	Am I the only person at this job who does anything to make things better?	PASSIVE	AGGRESSIVE	ASSERTIVE	PASSIVE-AGGRESSIVE

What do you think your communication style is? What makes you think this is your communication style?

_____

_____

_____

_____

_____

_____

_____

_____

_____

_____

_____

_____

_____

_____

_____

Understanding Your Wants and Needs with DEAR MAN

In this section, we'll explore the DEAR MAN skill as a method of understanding your wants and needs using a clear step-by-step method of communicating them. The acronym DEAR MAN equips you with the foundation skills needed to achieve respect for yourself as you offer the same to others when making a request. The steps in the acronym DEAR MAN are describe, express, assert, reinforce, mindful, appear confident, and negotiate.

Describe focuses on being aware of a situation that is based on facts, either from the past or present. Express includes opinion and perspectives related to the situation described to increase understanding. To assert is to be confident to ask, refuse, put safety measures in place, and enforce them in an emotionally balanced manner. The reinforce skill focuses on the objective of a win-win within the interaction. Being mindful is being aware when conversations are being shifted off-topic. It's important to stay focused and repeat requests when necessary. Appear confident allows you the opportunity to feel success and increases self-esteem and self-worth. The ability to negotiate gives you the opportunity to work through an issue collaboratively. In this way, you won't feel isolated and alone.

When using DEAR MAN, it's important to consider two effectiveness targets. The first is to think of the objective—what it is that you want to achieve. This is the target of the request you plan to discuss. The second is to identify why you are choosing the person you will be speaking with to meet your needs. It also sets a positive tone so that you and that person feel safe to communicate with each other.

Describe

In chapter 2, you learned about observation and description skills and how to use words to communicate what you're experiencing. The first step in using DEAR MAN is to describe. As you focus on describing a present situation or event in your life, you will use several of the skills you learned in the previous chapters. Describe focuses on the facts and also allows you to use a nonjudgmental stance to support clear, emotionally regulated information that is easy to understand, increasing your ability to be understood. This skill focuses on present moment communication so that you can begin to explain your perspective about what you may need and how you may feel about an experience in that moment.

Express

Expressing your perspectives, thoughts, and feelings adds to and supports the describe skill. Express connects the facts (objective information) with the introduction of your opinion about the facts (subjective information). Being clear and emotionally balanced when you express your opinion—including what you see and how you see a situation—can make this skill highly effective when making a request or clarifying your belief about things that have happened. It is key to consider that others can only understand what you share through your expression. This skill helps you be mindful of what you say and how you express yourself so that you're clearly communicating your needs.

"I" Can Express Myself

You've learned that expressing yourself when making a request and explaining in nonjudgmental language is highly effective when using the DEAR MAN skill. Let's practice working through a current situation that you may want to communicate to someone in your life. Answer each of the questions using the express skill, focusing on "I" statements.

"I" statements focus on the first person—and that's you! It is a healthier way to speak about your needs and feelings. Although it may seem selfish, it is not. Be brave and assertive when using the first person. It is safe to ask for what you need, so give yourself time to practice relearning how to speak in this way.

1. Describe the situation using facts in a few sentences.

2. Express how the situation makes you feel, using "I" statements. Consider ways you have been impacted by the situation and use the emotion words you have learned so far.

3. After you complete the exercise, reflect on how it feels to focus on communicating in this manner.

Assert

Now that you've learned the describe and express components, it's important to present these skills in a well-balanced and effective way. The assert skill is how we communicate facts and objective information. Asserting your wishes and wants, and doing so with confidence, is the focus of this skill. When we feel fearful or insecure, our communication relies on passive-aggressive words, including *should*, *would*, or *could*. In this skill, we also offer reasons we want what we want or need what we need. It's important to clearly state what you desire or to say no firmly. It's equally important to allow others to do the same, so you can learn to withstand being asked to respect a boundary or to meet the needs of a loved one.

Reinforce

Reinforcing what has been stated or asked of another is the next step in ensuring that you and the person you asked can find satisfaction in meeting the request. Reinforcing communication means finding the win-win in the interaction. When we present the facts and perspectives and identify how both parties can win, the likelihood that the outcome will work out increases and the communication is respectful. Know there is no guarantee that you will get what you want, but you will get what you need—which is respect and being able to work through strong urges to avoid confrontation. Focusing on your win just by communicating effectively means you will win every time, so reinforce your ability to use this skill.

Find the Win-Win

In the following exercise, you will read two scenarios and identify the win-win to lock in what is being requested. Look at your choices and think about what reinforced the satisfaction in each request. Suggested answers are in the back of the workbook (see page 165).

1. Helen has been in DBT group therapy for six months and has decided to speak with her therapist about only attending individual DBT psychotherapy. She has been managing her stress but feels insecure about how to use the reinforce skill to get the therapist to see it as a win-win. What recommendations would you suggest to Helen as a win-win to have her needs met?

2. Theo is prepared to return to work after experiencing PTSD symptoms for several months following an accident in his community. He admits that his confidence is low and wants to ask for an accommodation until he feels stable at work. What recommendations would you suggest to Theo as a win-win to have his needs met?

Mindful

Being mindful is a pivotal part of the DEAR MAN skill and is similar to the mindfulness skills in the first module. Staying mindful with communication focuses on being grounded with requests and uses objective effectiveness. That means you won't be distracted or change your position to get your point across to others.

When using the skill, strategies can keep you focused on your intention. One example is "the broken record," or repeating and restating your request or assertion. This is a skill that you want to be careful about overusing since it may be offensive if used too frequently or with an inappropriate tone. Being aware of how you express—and how others are responding to you expressing yourself—is also an important part of using this type of mindfulness.

Appear Confident

When communicating, it's important to be mindful of how you speak to others. Your volume, tone, and rate of speech are indicators of how others may perceive you. When we are agitated or unsure, our speech shows our insecurities and our nonverbal cues give the message that we are not confident and sure of what we're saying. Hesitating, repeating words and phrases, or looking away while speaking are signs that you may not be sure about yourself or what you need and want. Nonverbal cues can be difficult to master, especially for people who are neurodiverse, so it's important to find the behaviors that work best for you. Appearing confident increases clarity and manages trauma symptoms when you are focused, intentional, and mindful of what and how you're expressing your thoughts and feelings.

Increasing Confidence

Now it's time to test your confidence. During the next seven days, use your observation and description skills to identify ways you were able to appear confident. This is an exercise in awareness and to help you understand what you may need to correct on your own or with your therapist. When you have completed the table, reflect on what you have discovered about your confidence and how you plan to make changes.

| | MY CONFIDENCE | |
	Observation and Description	Notes for the Day
Sunday		
Monday		
Tuesday		
Wednesday		
Thursday		
Friday		
Saturday		

Use the lines below to reflect on any changes you want to make, things you may need support with changing, and what you discovered about how you express confidence to others.

....

....

....

Negotiate

The negotiation skill allows you to find a balance between what you are willing to offer and what you are willing to receive in relationships. This skill allows you to find ways of working with others to feel successful, while identifying alternative or collaborative solutions to problems or conflicts. The skill supports use of assertiveness, saying no, and being mindful of yourself and others when needed in a relationship.

PTSD symptoms may be a barrier to finding ways to negotiate and to finding many solutions to one problem. But when you practice this skill, you will find that you have more control with boundaries, which may increase your ability to feel safe enough to enforce them and to work collaboratively to solve problems when you need help.

The Art of Negotiation

Choose the most effective collaborative solution based on the negotiation prompt in italics for each situation. The answer key is in the back of the workbook (see page 165).

1. Sonia has decided to return to school, and her partner has expressed concern about the financial strain on their family. What is the most effective solution so Sonia can *focus on what will work*?

   a. Sonia will need to sacrifice for the family.

   b. The family will need to cut back on expenses so Sonia can live her dream.

   c. Sonia will sit with the family and ask for other solutions.

2. Cora has been asked on a date several times by a coworker and has said no several times, but now feels that the only way to make the coworker stop is to go on the date and "get it over with." What is the most effective way Cora can *find another solution to this problem*?

   a. Meet with a supervisor to report the coworker's behavior.

   b. Speak with a friend and take their advice.

   c. Shout at the coworker, "Leave me alone, for the hundredth time!"

3. Dana wants to take a vacation with his best friend, who wants to discuss a location and time to secure their plans. Dana feels anxious making decisions and can't stop worrying about what to do. What is the most effective solution so Dana can *stop worrying about what choice to make*?

   a. Dana can avoid his best friend and stop returning calls.

   b. Dana may need medication to deal with the anxiety.

   c. Dana may need to allow the friend to make the choice.

Validation Skills

While we know validation is an important part of interpersonal relationships, we also can acknowledge the complexity of the validation skill. As we continue to work on validating ourselves while doing the same for others, we can identify additional methods of how to do it to better our relationship effectiveness. Validation skills increase your ability to connect in relationships.

The first is making sure you focus and pay attention to what is being said. The next one is reflecting back content and emotional expression with focus on specific keywords that can offer insight into the important issues in discussions. Identifying unspoken nonverbal cues using the third skill, reading minds, keeps you aware of how communication is progressing and offers an opportunity to acknowledge and use nonverbals to show interest. For example, we frequently nod our heads when we hear something we agree with or can relate to, which offers the safe space to say something that further connects you.

Next is seeking to understand common emotions and human experiences and then acknowledging the valid experiences that fit the facts of a situation, which furthers relatability among all humans. Lastly, you want to have radical genuineness. This is achieved by connecting with others and avoiding minimizing or magnifying yourself or another person's experiences. Validation starts with you, so be yourself genuinely and authentically!

Pay Attention

Appearing interested is the key to what we have learned so far. Paying attention adds mindfulness to the skill use. As we practice appearing interested, we are focusing on the person speaking. This requires intention and being mindful of what we are doing, thinking, or feeling. Emotion regulation may be necessary when you're feeling bored by a discussion. Dividing your attention, with the goal of multitasking, is a barrier to validating and actively listening to what is being said. You can see the significance of paying attention in order to make this skill work and to empower you to use additional skills to support its effectiveness.

Barriers to Paying Attention

Use the following chart to identify your barriers to paying attention. There's an example for each of the categories that were identified during the explanation of the skill. Feel free to add other categories in the margins. Use the chart to work on being more attentive in your interactions with those in your life.

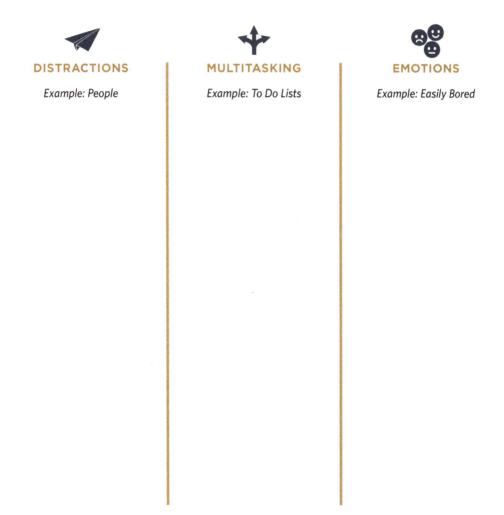

DISTRACTIONS	MULTITASKING	EMOTIONS
Example: People	*Example: To Do Lists*	*Example: Easily Bored*

Reflect Back

The ability to reflect and repeat exactly what another person is saying requires concentration, attentiveness, focus, and advanced skill use. Reflecting back is like you are a mirror facing the speaker so that they can see and hear what they're saying. This skill also helps you validate your ability to hear and understand by using the same words that are said.

The key aspect of this skill is to be genuine with your reflection; otherwise this is called *parroting* and may be considered offensive, hurtful, or perceived as if you're mocking what's being said. Be mindful of your tone, offer compassion, use nonjudgmental volume, and express concern following your reflection.

Reflection Connection

During the next week, practice seeing yourself and connecting with your own reflection in a mirror. Look at your own reflection and connect with your own image. Follow the steps below to recall the experience of focusing on yourself as you work on the goal of reflecting in a new way with others.

1. Find a safe space where you can give your full attention to this exercise.

2. Once you have identified your safe space, plan a time when you can work through each step.

3. When you are ready to begin the exercise, take a minute or two to close your eyes and quiet your mind to clear all mental and emotional distractions.

4. Gently open your eyes and look at yourself for 15 to 30 seconds as you observe all the parts of your face.

5. When you are ready, state one goal, intention, or feeling you have.

6. As you continue to look at your image, take a moment to mentally take in what you have said.

7. Then restate the goal, intention, or feeling.

8. As you look at yourself, look at the parts of your face and notice any changes that have occurred as a result of listening to yourself and reflecting your thoughts.

9. Feel free to journal this experience and to reflect on how it makes you think and feel about reflecting during your next communication with a loved one.

Read Minds

Validating using the read minds skill is to offer kindness and sensitivity with interpersonal experiences. As you have learned with the reflecting exercise, it's important to pay attention to shifts and changes in facial expressions, body language, what is happening in the environment, and what you think you know about the person with whom you are communicating. Being kind and compassionate shows that you are able and willing to express your understanding verbally or with action.

With this skill, it's important to ask questions and avoid making assumptions about what you think may be happening. If you feel unsure about what you think you are experiencing, gently let go of the thought or feeling and stay present to gather further observations.

Mind Reading

Using the observational skills you learned from the reflection exercise, work through an interpersonal interaction with one person this week. Pay attention to the changes in the expression of the person, whether the environment shifts, and how you are responding. When you are finished using your skill, assess what you need to work on as you move forward with increased interpersonal effectiveness.

Understand

Being able to understand another person requires nonjudgment and a willingness to be open and identify ways to connect that may be unclear. Using observation, active listening, and offering compassion while being present, you will be equipped to connect through experiences and things that are common to each of us as human beings.

Find things that make sense or emotions that you may have felt that are similar. Consider any vulnerabilities that others have, including current state of mind or emotion, as well as any physical concerns that may affect thoughts and emotions. As you learn to understand, you will find more opportunities to make sense of things and to connect with others in a more meaningful way.

Do I Seek to Understand?

Below are 10 statements that will help you identify where you may need to get better at connecting. For each of the questions below, answer TRUE or FALSE.

1.	I judge first and then describe what I experience.	TRUE	FALSE
2.	I focus on others before I focus on my own needs.	TRUE	FALSE
3.	I question the motives of people when I am asked for a favor.	TRUE	FALSE
4.	I go with the flow when plans change.	TRUE	FALSE
5.	I don't always have to be right.	TRUE	FALSE
6.	I can be in the present when someone speaks to me.	TRUE	FALSE
7.	I focus on what I need to say while someone is speaking.	TRUE	FALSE
8.	My emotions seem to control me in social settings.	TRUE	FALSE
9.	I feel compassion for those less fortunate than I am.	TRUE	FALSE
10.	I am compelled to give to alleviate my guilt and shame.	TRUE	FALSE

Reflect on how you may need to shift or where you are doing well. There is no right or wrong answer to these statements, but there are clear indicators of how you can make changes using interpersonal effectiveness skills. You make the choice to do better with your relationships.

Acknowledge the Valid

It can be difficult to make sense of communication that is distressing or upsetting or that doesn't make sense to you. As you work on using this skill by acknowledging the valid, some statements are understandable because they are a logical response to current facts.

By observing the truth of how a person's feelings, thinking, or actions are valid responses, you will find that aspects fit current facts where you can find understanding. Like the validation skills that you have and are learning, this skill requires openness, honesty, and compassion.

Validity Ability

We know that there are times in relationships when acknowledging the thoughts, feelings, and statements that we hear is challenging. The ability to find truth and facts gives you the confidence to regulate your emotions and to find the validity in spite of what you think about what is being said. Read through each statement on the left and seek to increase your validity ability in each item.

Statement	What is valid in this statement?
"You're upsetting me."	
"I just want to get along, but you make it so hard."	
"Let's just call it quits."	
"I feel hurt and have the urge to stop doing this."	
"Why do you always question everything I do?"	
"You are the most selfish person I know."	
"Why don't you want to spend time with me?"	
"I don't like the way you treat me."	
"I need you to be there for me."	
"Will you ever change?"	

Radical Genuineness

Your final validation skill focuses on you embracing being genuine and authentically yourself. This requires you to offer kindness, openness, and compassion to both yourself and others.

The key to this skill is to just be your wonderful self. You have learned how to be wonderful to others throughout this chapter, and now it's time to remember that you are important and are able to just be you. There is no longer a need to compare or to present yourself as more than or less than others.

Find what is equal, fair, and just with your relationships. This ensures that you and those you choose to communicate with are interacting with equal footing and are considered competent. Focus on finding that equal standing to avoid feeling inferior or incompetent.

Equal, Radical, Genuine

As you consider that you are genuine and can be an equal with others, and you become more authentic and safer in your life, this exercise will give you the space to explore this idea. On the lines that follow, respond to the prompts and explore, in the most radical way you can, how you are worthy of fairness and equality.

I believe I am an equal in these safe spaces:

_____

_____

_____

_____

_____

I know that I can be authentically myself with these people:

_____

_____

_____

_____

_____

continued

continued from page 131

I have experienced fairness in this way:

_____

_____

_____

_____

_____

I know that I am genuine in these experiences:

_____

_____

_____

_____

_____

Additional Interpersonal Effectiveness Skills for PTSD

As you work toward putting all your skills together, it's important to consider how to communicate these skills. In this section, we'll look at how to agree to disagree using validation. The idea of this may seem odd and, like many of the skills you have learned, difficult to imagine how to use. But you have learned how to be open and have tested things you were unable to figure out on your own, and now you're ready for a way to offer and to give respect.

Self-respect effectiveness and relationship effectiveness are what we will work on in order to make this happen. We need to offer safety and ease to others while we are honest. It's important to identify your values, priorities, and goals to keep communication honest and balanced.

Validation creates understanding, and being interested in what others are saying gives you another framework to achieve a new level of being understood. The benefit of using these skills is that you will feel safer asking for what you need and negotiating using the interpersonal effectiveness skills you learned earlier in this chapter. As you use these additional skills with all that you have learned so far, you will likely eliminate the need for avoidance and distraction with uncomfortable situations and step confidently into discussions that you once avoided or feared. By participating in this way, you will reinforce a new, balanced way of living. As you keep progressing toward the end of this chapter and this workbook, you will be more assertive with your skill use and will see that managing your PTSD symptoms is easier than you ever imagined.

Validating When You Disagree

It is often difficult to understand the important people in your life when you discover you have a disagreement with them. It can also be upsetting or frightening when you disagree with those you do not know. The ability to find truth or what is valid in disagreements allows you the ability to be assertive and to be respectful interpersonally as you work through the stress of strong emotions. Validation does not mean you agree with what is being said or challenged by another person, but rather allows the safe space for understanding by acknowledging that you understand why the person is disagreeing. It also creates an opportunity to ask for more information to better understand why there is a disagreement.

Agree to Disagree

Below is a list of 10 experiences that you can choose from that may cause a disagreement. Identify two of them and use validation to create understanding in the experience. Reflect on what it feels like to work through a disagreement using this skill.

1. Offer a different opinion about a television show.

2. State a differing opinion regarding a meal.

3. Ask someone to lower their voice.

4. Request a discount at a local store.

5. Ask for help cleaning from someone who has never helped you.

6. Request a change of topic while speaking to another person.

7. Assert your perspective to someone who you sense is disagreeable.

8. Order a special meal when others are ordering the same items.

9. Challenge a person's belief on a safe topic.

10. Go against what you think you know about one person.

Using GIVE

GIVE focuses on offering respect to others in order to make relationships stronger and to work toward establishing healthier, new relationships. The acronym stands for gentle, interested, validate, and easy manner. Being genuine means being authentically you with sincerity. Appearing interested in what others are saying signals that you care. Being able to validate the feelings and thoughts of others is an expression of empathy and compassion. Finally, easy manner is the way you can express kindness and approachability in your communication. GIVE creates a safe space to communicate with others.

GENTLE

Be gentle in communication. The way you speak—including tone, volume, and language—allows for effective communication. Being even-tempered and focusing on how information is conveyed increases your ability to regulate emotions and avoid harmful and threatening language, especially as you manage PTSD symptoms.

INTERESTED

Appearing interested, even if you are not, allows for emotional control and use of mindfulness skills. This skill allows you to develop patience and self-control as you work on calming emotions. Being authentically interested may be a consequence of acting or appearing interested. When you allow time to hear another person, you can gain perspective and factual information that may help you understand what the other person is communicating.

VALIDATE

Validation includes an awareness and acknowledgment of how another person is feeling, with or without words. Nodding or stating openly that you are hearing what is said is a sign that you understand what is being said. The benefit is increased compassion and empathy and an opportunity to connect with another person. The result is better relationships and greater use of your nonjudgment skill.

EASY MANNER

During difficult topics of conversation, being pleasant and having an ease in your manner makes things easier to say and hear. Smiling can allow you to connect without words before you speak and may give you a sense of safety within yourself and with the person who is listening to what is being said.

Take It Easy

For this exercise, you will need to find a trustworthy person in your life who you will see frequently during a one-week period and who is willing to offer constructive feedback without judgment. This is a test of your interpersonal effectiveness skills and emotion regulation skills. Ask your trusted person to observe and describe ways you are communicating with or without an easy manner. Validate what is being said and discuss ways you can improve your easy manner based on your discussion. Use the prompts and blank lines below to reflect on what you have learned about this experience.

1. My trustworthy person is: _____

2. The feedback I received was:

   _____

   _____

   _____

   _____

3. I felt this emotion when I was given this feedback:

   _____

   _____

   _____

   _____

4. My response to the feedback was:

   _____

   _____

   _____

   _____

5. What I thought about the feedback I received:

_____

_____

_____

_____

6. I wanted to (or had the urge to):

_____

_____

_____

_____

7. I validated the feedback by:

_____

_____

_____

_____

8. I plan to improve my easy manner by:

_____

_____

_____

_____

Using FAST

FAST focuses on your self-respect and allows you to have assertive and confident interactions. The acronym stands for fair, apologies not needed, stick to your values, and truthfulness. Being fair allows you to be respectful to yourself as you offer the same to others. Apologizing when it's unnecessary decreases your self-worth and is a habit to avoid. It's important to know that you only need to apologize when you have offended another person to increase self-respect. Being aware of values and sticking with them guides communication and what you feel is important to express. Lastly, practice honesty about what you want. The goal of FAST is to empower you to say what you need and want to say safely.

FAIR

Being fair when attempting to resolve an interpersonal conflict helps balance the differences in perspectives about a situation to find a solution that satisfies both sides. It may be challenging if you believe you are giving in, but there is always give-and-take in relationships, which is the key to using this skill effectively.

(NO) APOLOGIES

Although offering an apology is a sign of respect when we offend another person, this skill focuses on apologizing when it is appropriate. Habitual apologizing or over-apologizing for offenses that are out of context diminishes your self-worth. It's more helpful to be mindful of your offenses and when and if you need to apologize.

STICK TO YOUR VALUES

The ability to identify and to live by your values increases sound decision-making and safety in relationships. In stressful situations, or when another person challenges your values, having the ability to share your values helps you assert yourself to avoid compromise when it is unnecessary.

TRUTHFUL

Being honest, while sticking with your values, increases self-respect. Intentionally lying, avoiding telling the entire truth, or omitting details due to fear decreases self-respect and challenges the ability for others to trust you in relationships. Being truthful and working through the difficulties in thought or emotions increases interpersonal effectiveness.

Examining My Values

In this exercise, you will examine your values and consider how these values relate to your ability to being truthful in relationships.

Values include your morals, beliefs, and things that affect your decision-making. Justice, humanity, spirituality, nature, and love are all examples of values.

Think of five values that you have and write one on the first line next to each number below. Once you identify your values, write two ways you practice these values in your life. Then self-reflect if you are being true to these values with yourself and with others.

1. ....
....
....

2. ....
....
....

3. ....
....
....

4. ....
....
....

5. ....
....
....

Using GIVE and FAST Together

We all have disagreements and problems with relationships and need a way to work through them. As we work toward the end of this chapter, it's important to put these skills together. You have learned how to communicate with truthfulness while sticking to your values and using validation with an easy manner, so now let's connect these skills to achieve mutual respect.

To effectively use DEAR MAN with GIVE and FAST, you must begin with mindfulness using your wise mind. GIVE will ensure that you have effectiveness, and your request will be easier to understand and validate. Always consider context and timing as you work through your DEAR MAN. As you continue through each step, be sure to use FAST to stay assertive with your perspective.

Putting It All Together

Now we will practice and put DEAR MAN, GIVE, and FAST together. In this exercise, you will identify a problem or disagreement that needs a discussion, resolution, or negotiation. Perhaps you have been avoiding an issue, but you now have the skills to prepare, which is the intention of this exercise.

What is your objective effectiveness?

What is your interpersonal effectiveness?

Describe the situation

Express

continued

continued from page 141

Assert

Reinforce/Reward

Mindful

Appear Confident

Negotiate

Gentle

Interested

Validate

Easy Manner

Fair ....

....

Apologies not needed ....

....

Stick to your values ....

....

Truthful ....

....

Now that you have planned how to use DEAR MAN, GIVE, and FAST, plan to address this issue with the person you have avoided speaking with about the issue.

Key Takeaways

You have done a great job working on four modules of DBT! You have worked on connecting with others and managing your distress and emotional responses so that you can meet your needs as you achieve balance in your life. Let's look at the highlights of what you have done:

- You have learned interpersonal effectiveness and how to better your relationships.

- You understand how interpersonal effectiveness includes how you communicate and how others communicate with you.

- You learned how to have your wants and needs met using DEAR MAN, working through each step with openness and a greater ability to negotiate and safely compromise without surrendering.

- You learned ways to validate others and yourself.

- You learned to be more compassionate, kind, and understanding of others, while being the best you that you are.

- You no longer compare yourself to others and have learned to neither minimize nor magnify your position.

- You used the two supporting DEAR MAN skills, GIVE and FAST, to ensure that you offer respect and understand that you are worthy of respect.

- You learned how to offer and receive respect in spite of stress, distress, and fear.

- You have done amazing work, and those you love and who love you will benefit from all you have learned in this chapter!

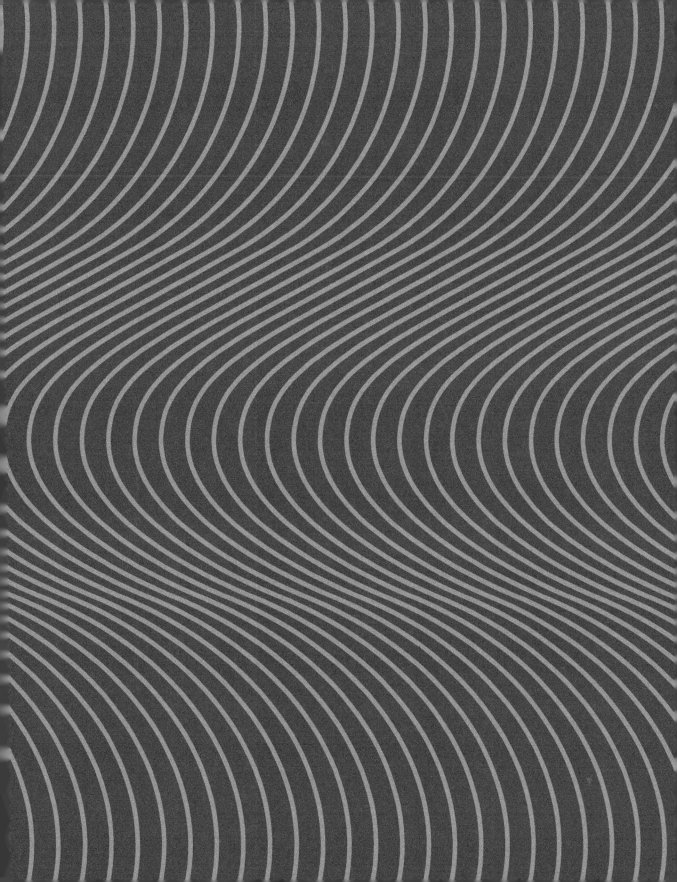

CHAPTER 6

Putting It All Together with DBT Prolonged Exposure Treatment

I have given myself permission to take risks with things that once frightened me. I am equipped to confront new situations and experiences with all that I now understand.

In this chapter, you will learn about DBT prolonged exposure (PE) treatment as a method of resolving distress related to traumatic events and gaining a sense of control when having a traumatic response. We'll begin with an explanation of prolonged exposure treatment, focusing on its history and how it may benefit the four modules of DBT. We'll then learn the stages of prolonged exposure, and you'll complete a self-evaluation to determine your readiness for PE.

This final chapter will break down the exposure steps of PE treatment, with real-life examples to show how it helps PTSD and how the treatment works. To conclude, you will become familiar with what a relapse prevention plan is, how it works, and why it is important to manage PTSD. Moving forward, you will learn to live a life without fear of exposure to traumatic situations from your past and why the PE steps can help you secure your stability as you prepare to move forward on your life's journey.

What Is Prolonged Exposure Treatment?

Prolonged exposure (PE) treatment was developed by Dr. Marsha Linehan to address the trauma of people diagnosed with borderline personality disorder. A prolonged exposure treatment plan is offered after the four modules of DBT are understood and easily used to deal with distress and emotional dysregulation. As you have learned all four of the DBT modules in this workbook, you may consider facing the traumatic event that has contributed to your PTSD. Prolonged exposure with a structured DBT treatment plan continues to be used when working through the root causes of trauma. It also helps identify many of the factors related to avoidance and distress due to a traumatic event that may keep you stuck in a vulnerable state of traumatization.

Prolonged exposure treatment is commonly used with other mental health diagnoses, such as generalized anxiety disorder (GAD), obsessive-compulsive disorder (OCD), or phobic disorders. You may have heard of people who are afraid of spiders who are gradually exposed to a visual or an actual spider in order to overcome the fear. The goal of using a prolonged exposure approach is to minimize the level of distress and panic that may be experienced when revisiting a trauma narrative as you work to function at a more emotionally controlled level.

Prolonged exposure treatment is based on cognitive behavioral therapy (CBT) and gives a more structured approach to traumatic memories, feelings, and events. This approach works step-by-step as you gradually expose yourself to thoughts and experiences that once resulted in a loss of control and PTSD symptoms. Prolonged exposure treatment supports you as you take these steps within the safety of a therapeutic environment. You will work to increase your ability to withstand strong emotions and to manage the distressing recall of the traumatic situation as you regulate emotions and fear loses its power.

The Basics of DBT PE

In this section, we'll review the basics of DBT PE treatment before exploring each of the three stages individually. As we previously discussed, PE is gradual in its approach to working through trauma using a planned system of exposure to a trigger. It involves recalling a traumatic event to confront the cause or person related to the trauma. Prolonged exposure can last for a total of 15 weekly therapy sessions with a duration of 60 to 120 minutes per session. The duration depends on the treatment plan and the time needed to process the experience related to the exposure. DBT PE begins with a discussion of the details of the treatment, how it will be planned, and what skills you need in order to manage the emotional responses that may occur using distress tolerance skills. Therapy will begin based on the treatment plan as you discuss and eventually expose the traumatic memories and situations that resulted in PTSD.

STAGE 1

During the first stage of PE treatment, you'll develop an understanding of the benefits and risks of using this treatment. This stage is called *pre-exposure*, as it sets a safe and clear awareness of what is going to happen before any treatment begins. This allows for a better sense of choice and autonomy in the treatment-planning stage and can give you the time to ask questions and examine your readiness before exposing yourself to any possible harm. This is important to know since it is an ethical boundary that a DBT psychotherapist must adhere to in order to keep you safe. An example of this process is that you will discuss your consent and will explore how prolonged exposure may help and how it may cause undue harm. This is typically done in writing during the treatment-planning phase and is frequently discussed throughout the course of treatment. When you decide to consent, you can expect to share details of the trauma, create a plan to cope with trauma activation, also referred to as "triggers," and create a plan to gradually expose the trauma with in-vivo trauma-related cues.

STAGE 2

During the second stage of DBT PE, a more active phase of treatment begins. As part of treatment planning, you'll discuss the exploration of the traumatic event or situations related to the event as you work on the goal of identifying a hierarchy for exposure. You can visualize this as a ladder, with the lower-level traumatic events climbing to more intense events. Once informed consent is established, you can expect to share details of the trauma narrative and to create and review the exposure plan you developed to manage trauma activation and to discuss any necessary changes to effectively move through the experience. During this phase, you will work through the exposure plan, gradually exposing the trauma narrative. You will explore and identify the emotions, behaviors, thoughts, and physical symptoms of the narrative and use your mind to recall the past, while being supported by your therapist to ensure your safety. This may include deep breathing or a guided meditation to help with grounding at the end of the sessions. This stage focuses on identifying symptoms related to the PTSD that cause distress, fear, and continued trauma.

STAGE 3

During the final stage of PE treatment, you will experience the most active phase of this therapy. This stage is called in-vivo ("real life") prolonged exposure, as it requires more activity outside the therapeutic environment. As with the prior stage, the exposure is structured to target the PTSD symptoms with similar situations related to the experience that the trauma activates. An example may be having a fear of dogs after being attacked by one during childhood. After exploring the hierarchy of exposure—which might include seeing a picture of a dog as a first step, then exploring the physical pain, rehabilitation, the fear of being attacked again, and the nightmares recalling the sound of hearing dogs growling—you may eventually go to a kennel to see an actual dog. This is an example of the connection between the three stages. The challenge with this stage of therapy is that it requires action without the immediate support of a therapist. At this stage, it is expected that DBT skill use is part of a well-structured routine and sets a safe and clear awareness of what is going to happen before any treatment begins.

Evaluation: Are You Ready for DBT PE?

Now let's examine your readiness for taking the step toward living an exposure lifestyle. Review the 10 statements below and select either TRUE or FALSE.

I have a distress tolerance plan.	TRUE	FALSE
I have a DBT-certified therapist.	TRUE	FALSE
I have completed the exercises in this workbook.	TRUE	FALSE
I want to face my fears.	TRUE	FALSE
I am frightened and scared of doing this level of therapy.	TRUE	FALSE
I have a recurring memory that keeps me from functioning at my best.	TRUE	FALSE
I avoid illegal drugs, alcohol, and other addictive substances.	TRUE	FALSE
I am comfortable with the idea of being uncomfortable if it helps me to be better.	TRUE	FALSE
I feel stronger as a result of doing the exercises in this workbook.	TRUE	FALSE
I will use the skills I have learned while finding a DBT-certified therapist to continue my journey forward.	TRUE	FALSE

If your responses are TRUE to all of these statements, you are ready to take this step. Being frightened is normal, and having a plan and a qualified person to support you is important. Facing fears soberly increases your strength and confidence. The fact that you did the skills in this workbook proves you do not quit, so keep moving forward!

How DBT PE Works

Imaginal exposure is the start of DBT PE, and the name identifies a bit of how it works and what will happen. You will begin to use your imagination to remember and expose the traumatic event, any of the associated emotions, and other details that are related to the trauma. At the beginning of imaginal exposure, a gradual plan (also called a hierarchy) will be introduced to identify the levels of trauma to be addressed. Some people may choose to journal memories or flashbacks as they are activated during the start of treatment to begin this process. For others, there may be one single experience that has been the most difficult to overcome, and there may be no hierarchy, but rather a gradual exposure to one memory. There is no right or wrong way to approach a memory or a traumatic recall.

As you work through your narrative, you may identify symptoms related to PTSD. An example may be flashbacks that challenge sleep or an overwhelming fear in the presence of an offender. The details of the event may also include behaviors or physical symptoms, avoidance, negative thoughts, mood disturbances, and arousal responses. Examples include dissociation, physical sensations related to trauma, memory problems, blaming, isolation, poor concentration, and reckless, aggressive, or irritable behaviors.

Establishing and using your distress tolerance plan becomes integral as you work through the details of how the trauma occurred and how it continues to affect your daily living. During an imaginal exposure therapy session, a therapist may use a guided meditation to work on activating one of the identified situations discussed if it is challenging to begin the process. As you work on identifying what needs to be addressed based on the PTSD symptoms that are lingering, you will gradually and safely be able to use your imagination to heal in a safe space. Once you are able to discover the problematic and persistent traumatic issues, you will be equipped for the new phase of DBT PE therapy.

Imaginal Exposure

Imaginal exposure is the start of a more active phase of PE treatment. After consent is agreed upon and there is a clearly understood plan of how to use prolonged exposure to help you work through PTSD, you will explore the narrative related to the trauma. The focus is on recalling and telling the story of the trauma and the emotions related to the experience with support from a therapist who is qualified to do this with you. This is where the benefit of a DBT-certified therapist gives you the safety needed because skill use is necessary to work through remembering distressing experiences. Through the process of exploring the past events associated with PTSD, you are offered encouragement, a plan, and awareness of how far you choose to explore. During sessions, you may discuss emotions, thoughts, behaviors, and physiological responses following the event and how you respond to similar situations or people who remind you of, or are a part of, the experience. Distress tolerance and emotion regulation skills are helpful during this stage of PE since there are often PTSD responses during recall.

In-Vivo Exposure

The final stage of prolonged exposure is stage 3, referred to as in-vivo exposure. This allows you to face experiences, people, and possibly fears related to a traumatic event. With in-vivo exposure, you will safely be able to confront those things that trigger or activate a response. Earlier in this chapter, we discussed triggers as things that activate a PTSD response. The goal with DBT is to use mindfulness to control the sights, sounds, smells, tastes, and sensations to change the activation from traumatic to a well-controlled experience that you can choose to participate in or to avoid with a distress tolerance skill. DBT, along with prolonged exposure, replaces the old response with a healthier, less fearful one as the mind learns a more emotionally balanced way to respond to those signals. With a DBT-certified therapist, you can create a plan for gradual and progressive in-vivo exposure as you work through challenging experiences outside of sessions and process the experience safely during individual therapy sessions.

Creating a Relapse Prevention Plan

To relapse is to return to a reduced state of functioning or to return to your prior state of functioning when making new changes in your life. As you conclude this workbook and after mastering DBT skill use, it is vital to reduce your vulnerability to relapse by developing a relapse prevention plan.

An effective plan to prevent relapse includes being aware of old thought patterns, behaviors, and emotions that increase in frequency and intensity. Negative thoughts frequently sabotage the success of a recovery plan, so it is important to care for your mind and to be mindful of what you allow to enter your mind. Writing a plan and using the exercises from this workbook are a good start to ensure you have a written document to easily refer to when distressed or fearful. A relapse prevention plan should include a list of vulnerabilities, including people, places, situations, and things that may trigger old ways of functioning. It is equally important to write DBT skills that work for you, emergency numbers, and a list of resources. You can find helpful resources at the end of this workbook.

Living an Exposure Lifestyle

The ability to live an exposure lifestyle means having a sense of control when experiencing situations that once resulted in distress. As you work through prolonged exposure, the need to withstand and process events that are traumatic or those that may remind you of prior trauma lessens and, for some, may go away altogether. For those with PTSD, a life of freedom from flashbacks and fear creates improved daily functioning, confidence, and the ability to make more effective decisions. With less reactivity and a greater understanding of what healthy reactions to a variety of stressful situations look and feel like, the tendency to avoid and distract from stressors is minimal.

The thing to consider as you live without fear of exposure to traumatic situations is a newfound ability as a survivor who can face difficulties and has the ability to help others. As you learn to persevere, with hope and as an example of how to recover from trauma, you will identify the benefit in your story and continue to grow as an example of a most purposeful life.

Key Takeaways

You have completed the final chapter of this workbook. As we finish this part of our journey together, understand that you will now have a new beginning. Before you do, let's look at the summary of your key takeaways from chapter 6:

- You learned the basics of DBT PE and how it may be useful to you.

- You increased your awareness of PE with real-life examples to help identify your readiness for treatment with a brief quiz.

- You explored the two active phases of the DBT PE process with an explanation of the benefits.

- You now have a clearer understanding of how to work through safe exposure to similar triggers to overcome PTSD.

- You know the stages of DBT PE in detail and how to ensure your safety if you choose to use this treatment.

- You are now prepared to use DBT to overcome your trauma narrative and have concluded this beautiful first step in your wonderful new life.

- You have learned and mastered what is needed to move forward and heal the trauma. Congratulations!

Your Journey Forward

You have made it to the end of your journey, and now it's time to summarize all you have completed in this workbook. You have learned how to function in mindfulness, manage distress, regulate and understand your emotions, and have healthier relationships while learning to express your needs and wants. The exercises that you completed supported your ability to look at yourself and how you function in your world. The skills that you now have will allow you to function differently in an extraordinary and new way with awareness, acceptance, and action.

Continuing to use your skills and making them a part of your daily routine will further your recovery from PTSD, with prolonged exposure treatment and finding a DBT-certified therapist to help you along the way. As you complete these steps, there are a few additional aspects of recovery to consider that will support you as you move even further forward, gain control of your life, and feel stronger. Evidenced-based treatment methods can complement what you have learned with DBT and can take you to a new level of awareness in your recovery journey. Posttraumatic growth (PTG) is one method of exploring how to find a greater understanding that goes beyond the concept of acceptance that you learned when working through distress tolerance. When you are better able to prevent distress, exploring PTG may be a method of helping others and finding a greater purpose for your experience through action.

As you move forward with all that you have explored, learned, uncovered, and recovered from, I again congratulate you for doing this work—it took you working consistently to get to the end of this workbook. I encourage you to explore additional resources and to use this workbook again and again as you reflect on how far you have come in a short period of time. Acknowledge your progress, your struggles, and your ability to overcome, and, most important, that you chose to create an enjoyable life that far exceeds your trauma narrative. It has been an honor to support and offer you what I have learned personally and professionally as a way of increasing your ability to live mindfully, love, be loved thoughtfully, and be as amazing as I know you must be in order to make it to the end of this phase of your life's journey.

RESOURCES

Here is a list of websites, phone numbers, workbooks, and helpful tools to support you when you need help, when you want to offer help to others who are struggling, or if you want to explore and learn more.

Websites and Phone Numbers for Support, Crisis Intervention, and Information

American Psychological Association
APA.org/ptsd-guideline/treatments/prolonged-exposure

Copline
A 24-hour hotline for confidential calls with retired police officers.
1-800-267-5463 | Copline.org

Crisis Text Line
CrisisTextLine.org | Text BADGE to 741741

Narm Training Institute Transforming Trauma Podcast
NARMTraining.com/transformingtrauma

National Alliance on Mental Illness
NAMI.org
NAMI HelpLine (NAMI.org/Find-Support/NAMI-HelpLine) to find out what services and support are available in your community.

National Center for PTSD
PTSD.va.gov

National Suicide Prevention Lifeline
1-800-273-8255

RAINN
A resource for survivors of rape and incest.
RAINN.org

ResponderStrong
   A resource for police officers and firefighters.
   ResponderStrong.org

Stay Safe Foundation
   StaySafeFoundation.org

Trans Lifeline
   A resource by and for trans individuals.
   TransLifeline.org

The Trauma Foundation
   TheTraumaFoundation.org

The Trevor Project
   A resource for LGBTQIA+ youth.
   TheTrevorProject.org

Workbooks

Denborough, D. *Retelling the Stories of Our Lives: Everyday Narrative Therapy to Draw Inspiration and Transform Experience*. New York: Norton, 2014.

Heller, L. and A. LaPierre. *Healing Developmental Trauma: How Early Trauma Affects Self-Regulation, Self-Image, and the Capacity for Relationship*. Berkeley, CA: North Atlantic Books, 2012.

Linehan, M. M. *DBT Skills Training Handouts and Worksheets*. New York: The Guilford Press, 2014.

Pederson, L. and C. Pederson. *The Expanded Dialectical Behavior Therapy Skills Training Manual: DBT for Self-Help and Individual & Group Treatment Settings, 2nd Edition*. Eau Claire, WI: Premier Publishing and Media, 2017.

Schneiderman, K. *Step Out of Your Story: Writing Exercises to Reframe and Transform Your Life*. Novato, CA: New World Library, 2015.

Tedeschi, R. G. and B. A. Moore. *The Posttraumatic Growth Workbook: Coming Through Trauma Wiser, Stronger, and More Resilient*. Oakland, CA: New Harbinger Publications, 2016.

Tedeschi, R. G. and B. A. Moore. *Transformed by Trauma: Stories of Posttraumatic Growth.* Boulder Crest, 2020.

Van Der Kolk, B. *The Body Keeps the Score: Brain, Mind, and Body in the Healing of Trauma.* New York: Penguin Books, 2015.

World Health Organization. (2013). "Guidelines for the management of conditions specifically related to stress." Journals.PLOS.org/plosmedicine/article?id=10.1371/journal.pmed.1001769.

Zolli, A. and A. M. Healy. *Resilience: Why Things Bounce Back.* New York: Simon & Schuster, 2012.

REFERENCES

American Counseling Association. (2014). Code of ethics. Retrieved from Counseling.org/docs/ethics/2014-aca-code-of-ethics.pdf?sfvrsn=4.

American Psychiatric Association. (2013). *Diagnostic and Statistical Manual of Mental Disorders* (5th ed.). Washington, D.C.

American Psychological Association. (2020). *The Publication Manual of the American Psychological Association* (7th ed.). Washington, D.C.

Foa, E. B., C. V. Dancu, E. A. Hembree, L. H. Jaycox, E. A. Meadows, and G. P. Street. "A Comparison of Exposure Therapy, Stress Inoculation Training, and Their Combination for Reducing Posttraumatic Stress Disorder in Female Assault Victims." *Journal of Consulting and Clinical Psychology*, 67, 194–200. 1999.

Görg, N., J. R. Böhnke, K. Priebe, S. Rausch, S. Wekenmann, P. Ludäscher, M. Bohus, and N. Kleindienst. "Changes in Trauma-Related Emotions Following Treatment with Dialectical Behavior Therapy for Posttraumatic Stress Disorder after Childhood Abuse." *Journal of Traumatic Stress*, 32(5), 764–773. 2019. DOI.org/10.1002/jts.22440.

Harned, M. S. and M. Linehan. "Integrating Dialectical Behavior Therapy and Prolonged Exposure to Treat Co-occurring Borderline Personality Disorder and PTSD: Two Case Studies." *Cognitive and Behavioral Practice*, 15(3), 263–276. 2008. DOI.org/10.1016/j.cbpra.2007.08.006.

Harned, M. S., A. K. Ruork, J. Liu, and M. A. Tkachuck. "Emotional Activation and Habituation During Imaginal Exposure for PTSD Among Women with Borderline Personality Disorder." *Journal of Traumatic Stress*, 28(3). 2015. DOI.org/10.1002/jts.22013.

Harned, M. S., and S. C. Schmidt. "Integrating Post-Traumatic Stress Disorder Treatment into Dialectical Behaviour Therapy: Clinical Application and Implementation of the DBT Prolonged Exposure Protocol." In M. A. Swales (Ed.), *The Oxford Handbook of Dialectical Behaviour Therapy* (pp. 797–814). Oxford University Press, 2019.

Harned, M. S., L. A. Ritschel, and S. C. Schmidt. "Effects of Workshop Training in the Dialectical Behavior Therapy Prolonged Exposure Protocol on Clinician Beliefs, Adoption, and Perceived Clinical Outcomes." *Journal of Traumatic Stress, 34*(2). 2020. DOI.org/10.1002/jts.22622.

Hays, P. A. "Integrating Evidence-Based Practice, Cognitive-Behavior Therapy, and Multicultural Therapy: Ten Steps for Culturally Competent Practice." *Professional Psychology: Research and Practice, 40*(4), 354–360. 2009. DOI.org/10.1037/a0016250.

Jayawickreme, E., F. J. Infurna, K. Alajak, et al. (2020). "Post-traumatic Growth as Positive Personality Change: Challenges, Opportunities, and Recommendations." *Journal of Personality.* 00:1–21. DOI.org/10.1111/jopy.12591.

Jerud, A. B., F. J. Farach, M. Bedard-Gilligan, H., Smith, L. A. Zoellner, and N. C. Feeny. "Repeated Trauma Exposure Does Not Impair Distress Reduction During Imaginal Exposure for Posttraumatic Stress Disorder." 2016. DOI.org/10.1002/da.22582.

Linehan, M. M. *Cognitive Behavioral Treatment for Borderline Personality Disorder.* New York: The Guilford Press, 1993.

Linehan, M. M. *Skills Training Manual for Treating Borderline Personality Disorder.* New York: The Guilford Press, 1993.

Little, S. G., A. Akin-Little, and M. P. Somerville. "Response to Trauma in Children: An Examination of Effective Intervention and Post-Traumatic growth." *School Psychology International, 32*(5), 448–463. 2011. DOI.org/10.1177/0143034311402916.

Pederson, L. and C. A. Pederson. *The Expanded Dialectical Behavior Therapy Skills Training Manual: Practical DBT for Self-Help, and Individual & Group Treatment Settings.* Eau Claire, WI: Premier Publishing and Media, 2012.

Pitman, R. K., S. P. Or, B. Altman, R. E. Longpre, R. E. Poire, M. L. Macklin, M. J. Michaels, and G. S. Steketee. "Emotional Processing and Outcome of Imaginal Flooding Therapy in Vietnam Veterans with Chronic Posttraumatic Stress Disorder." *Comprehensive Psychiatry, 37*, 409—418. 1996.

Tol, W. A., C. Barbui, J. Bisson, J. Cohen, Z. Hijazi, L. Jones, et al. (2014). "World Health Organization Guidelines for Management of Acute Stress, PTSD, and Bereavement: Key Challenges on the Road Ahead." *PLoS Med, 11*(12): e1001769. DOI.org/10.1371/journal.pmed.1001769.

Weigold I., R. Boyle, A. Weigold, S. Antonucci, H. Mitchell, and C. Martin-Wagar. "Personal Growth Initiative in the Therapeutic Process: An Exploratory Study." *The Counseling Psychologist, 46*(4), 481–504. 2018. DOI.org/10.1177/0011000018774541.

ANSWER KEY

EXPLORING YOUR MIND WITH MINDFUL SOLUTIONS • 16

a-5; b-8; c-9; d-7; e-4; f-6; g-1; h-3; i-10; j-2

A STATE OF WISDOM • 24

Emotional mind: a, h, j

Rational mind: d, g

Wise mind: b, c, e, f, i

OBSERVING THE SENSES • 27

Asia is experiencing flashbacks of the assault and seems to be fighting her assailant.

THE SUPPORTIVE WHAT DETECTIVE • 28

It is helpful for Lynne to speak with her boss since she has a plan and a supportive therapist to work with her. Lynne has enough support in place as she takes steps to return to work and to manage her symptoms with minimal distress. Her decision to return is a wise mind choice as she works through her distress tolerance.

NONJUDGMENTAL LANGUAGE • 30

Judgmental (1, 2, 6, 7, 8, 9)

Nonjudgmental (3, 4, 5, 10)

OPPOSITE TO EMOTION • 96

1. Depressed/Joyful
2. Afraid/Certain
3. Bored/Interested
4. Confident/Insecure
5. Worried/Faithful
6. Scared/Brave
7. Shy/Expressive
8. Exhausted/Energized
9. Hysterical/Controlled
10. Jealous/Compassionate

UNDERSTANDING YOUR COMMUNICATION STYLE • 108

1. I feel tired and need a cup of tea. ASSERTIVE

2. I wish I had someone to take care of me. PASSIVE

3. Nobody ever asks me how I'm doing. PASSIVE

4. Everybody is out to get me. AGGRESSIVE

5. I can't believe no one cleaned this kitchen! AGGRESSIVE

6. I'm glad somebody understands me. ASSERTIVE

7. Whatever. PASSIVE-AGGRESSIVE

8. Who cares? PASSIVE-AGGRESSIVE

9. It is what it is. ASSERTIVE

10. Am I the only person at this job who does anything to make things better? PASSIVE-AGGRESSIVE

FIND THE WIN-WIN • 114

1. Helen can work with the therapist to create an updated treatment plan for individual therapy that includes a plan to step down from group sessions. The therapist will ensure Helen minimizes instability and has her needs met.

2. Theo can meet with the human resource department and supervisor for a return-to-work plan and a reasonable accommodation while transitioning to a consistent work schedule.

THE ART OF NEGOTIATION • 119

1. c

2. a

3. c

INDEX

PLEASE skills, 85–94
reappraising feelings, 99–100
self-soothing methods, 101–102
Encouragement (IMPOVE skill), 59, 60
Exercise (PLEASE skill), 93–94. *See also*
    Intense exercise (TIPP skill)
Exposure. *See* Prolonged exposure
    (PE) treatment
Express (DEAR MAN skill), 110, 111–112

F

Fair (FAST skill), 138
FAST skills, 138, 140–143
Flashbacks, 3

G

Gentle (GIVE skill), 135
Genuineness, radical, 130–132
GIVE skills, 135, 140–143

H

HOW skills, 15, 25, 29–31

I

Imagery (IMPROVE skill), 58
IMPROVE skills, 58–61
Intense exercise (TIPP skill), 67
Interested (GIVE skill), 135
Interpersonal effectiveness
    about, 8, 106
    acknowledging validity, 128–129
    benefits of, 107
    communication style, 108–109
    DEAR MAN skills, 110–119, 140–143
    FAST skills, 138, 140–143
    GIVE skills, 135–137, 140–143
    mind reading, 124–125
    paying attention, 120–121
    radical genuineness, 130–132
    reflecting back, 122–123

understanding, 126–127
validation skills, 120, 133–134, 136–137

L

Linehan, Marsha, 6, 148
Loving kindness, 29, 97–98

M

Making space, 32–34
Meaning (IMPROVE skill), 58, 61
Mind, states of
    about, 15
    emotional, 17–19
    rational, 20–22
    wise, 23–24
Mindful (DEAR MAN skill), 110, 116–117
Mindfulness
    about, 6–7, 12
    benefits of, 12–13
    HOW skills, 15, 25, 29–31
    making space, 32–34
    for negative self-talk, 16
    routines, 35–37
    WHAT skills, 15, 25–28
Mind reading, 124–125

N

Negotiate (DEAR MAN skill), 110, 118–119
Nonjudgmentally (HOW skill), 29, 30–31

O

Observation (WHAT skill), 25, 26, 27, 52
Observe (STOP skill), 55
One-mindfully (HOW skill), 29
One thing in the moment (IMPROVE skill), 59
Opposite to emotion/opposite action, 95–96

P

Paced breathing (TIPP skill), 67, 69
Paired muscle relaxation (TIPP skill), 67, 69

Acknowledgments

I want to thank all the brave souls who have crossed the threshold to my office and surrendered their pain to find a purposeful, new way of living. Trauma called me to this work and connected each of you with me, so nothing is a mistake but an opportunity to heal. I honor your willingness and ability to "do the work" despite what you have endured. Continue to move forward and live according to your own calling as I see the divine in each and every one of you.

About the Author

Dr. Victoria A. Wright, LPC, DBTC ("Dr. V"), is an educational psychologist, certified DBT psychotherapist, licensed professional counselor, certified guidance counselor, and on-site trauma consultant. Dr. Wright is the owner of Integrated Mental Health Services, LLC, and has been in private practice for more than 10 years. She currently serves as the secretary of the Pennsylvania College Counseling Association. She works with institutions to train future clinicians to address the significance of trauma and integrative care. Dr. Wright has published and presented at state conferences on issues related to race-based trauma, stereotype threat, and barriers to academic achievement.

CPSIA information can be obtained
at www.ICGtesting.com
Printed in the USA
LVHW072006160422
716388LV00016B/672

9 781638 784937